DHARMA AND DEVELOPMENT

Religions of Sri Lanka

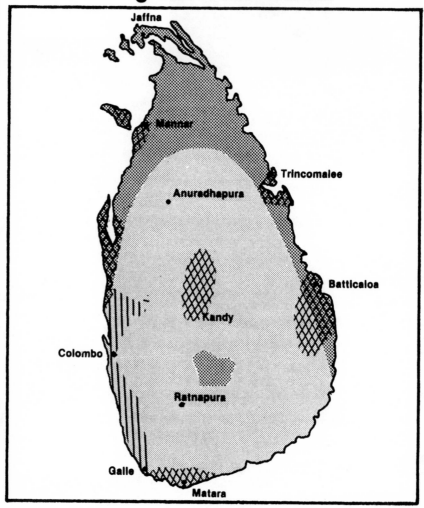

Religion		Percentage of Total Pop.	
▦	Predominantly Buddhist	68%	
▩	Predominantly Hindu	18%*	*11% Ceylonese Tamils, in the north
▨	Muslim concentrations	7%	7% "estate" Tamils, in Central Highlands
▥	Christian concentrations	7%	

DHARMA AND DEVELOPMENT

Religion as Resource in the Sarvodaya Self-Help Movement

Revised Edition

Joanna Macy

WITH AN INTRODUCTION BY
A. T. Ariyaratna, *Founder, President*
Sarvodaya Shramadana Movement

 KUMARIAN PRESS

Library of Congress Cataloging in Publication Data

Macy, Joanna, 1929-
  Dharma and development.

  Bibliography: p. 117
    1.Sarvodaya (Organization : Sri Lanka)
2. Buddhism and social problems—Sri Lanka.
3. Economic development—Religious aspects—Buddhism.
4. Women—Sri Lanka—Social conditions. 5. Sri Lanka
—Social conditions. I. Title.
HN40.B8M32   1985   261.8'3'095493   85-236
ISBN 0-931816-53-X

First printing 1983
Second (revised) printing 1985
Third printing 1988
Fourth printing 1989

Printed in the United States of America

Cover design by Marilyn Penrod

Contents

Foreword

Humanity faces a crisis of global dimensions. This is a crisis of survival for almost one billion of the poorest of the poor, and of recession, unemployment, unrest, and possibly war for all the rest. Values, and collective action based on values, have a crucial role to play: they can either turn crisis into catastrophe or reverse trends and create a positive, humane social and cultural transformation.

Joanna Macy's book shows one trend, one of the most hopeful, in collective action based on values appropriate to pull humanity out of the syndrome of breakdown and chaos. The developing countries, with their rich and still powerful historical and cultural heritage, have much to offer not only for themselves, but for the entire human community of the globe. The movement of Sarvodaya and its use of the Buddhist value-system (or the Dharma) in development are excellent examples. They are among the new ways of valuing, thinking, and acting that are needed; these have a role to play which is well-nigh unprecedented in history.

This role may be understood in terms of the dynamics of complex open systems. Human beings are such systems and so are human societies. In interaction with the environing world they stabilize and organize themselves as they sustain and evolve functional norms. Current economic, environmental, and social stresses—producing poverty and starvation, conflict and alienation, and sapping the will to live—threaten to destroy the balance of collective human systems that are normally self-stabilizing. If these are not to prove lethal to human physical survival, societies must evolve new norms and transform themselves. Fortunately, in such a period of critical instability, the systems' automatic or predetermined modes of self-correcting give way. A period of indeterminacy (or systemic freedom) begins, in which the system's values and choices play a determining role. These creative changes may be quite small initially, but can spread with great rapidity and, with a decisive initial "kick," launch social change in a specific direction.

This, then, is the central meaning and message of the Sarvodaya Movement so ably and faithfully described by Joanna Macy. It is a small movement that grows. From one village and a handful of high-school students working under the inspired guidance of a man of vision it has spread to a whole country, and now it is spreading to other countries. It is making its intellectual and moral imprint on the Western world as well. If conditions were "normal," with human systems operating in their natural semi-stable state, such a movement would remain a peripheral curiosity. But in the era into which we are now entering, a movement like this can have entirely unforeseen possibilities; it can become a key agent of change.

It is not likely that any one idea will gain global prominence; but as countless new ideas, and actions based on them, surface, they will move the giant structures and institutions of this planetary system into an entirely new dimension of functioning. Knowing more about the Sarvodaya Movement is thus important both in itself and for what it tells us of the ability of people and societies to create their own future and pull themselves out of the crisis that threatens to engulf the whole twentieth-century world.

This book should be read, then, for what it tells us of the potentials of one movement that fuses religion and tradition with pragmatism and innovation, and also for what it suggests of the ability of the human species to respond to crises and evolve to a new level of individual existence and social and cultural organization. We are entering an epoch of freedom of choice and innovation, and the seeds of the new world we can create include movements such as Sarvodaya and the ideas and actions arising from its application of Dharma to development.

ERVIN LASZLO
*Director of Programs on
Regionalism and the New Inter-
national Economic Order, United
Nations Institute for Training and
Research*

Preface

This book brings together two major preoccupations of my life which in earlier years seemed to pull me in opposing directions. Fascinated by the ultimate questions that our species asks itself about the nature of reality, I studied religion—first my own Judeo-Christian heritage and then others, especially Buddhism. Over the years, as I bore and raised my children, I frequented theologians, philosophers, monks, nuns, sadhus, and shamans, learned prayers in convents, meditation in Himalayan hermitages, and in libraries delved into comparative metaphysics. Yet all the while I was equally drawn to the more mundane questions of how people in groups hurt and exploit one another, and of how some find the courage to right social wrongs. So I studied political science, too, from Locke to Marx to anarchism, worked in the State Department, the Peace Corps, and the Urban League, and spent long hours and days with colleagues in movements for civil rights, prison reform, safe energy, and peace. Back and forth I went between these two poles of life, the spiritual and the political: from meditating to public speaking, from preparing testimony on nuclear waste to reading Sanskrit texts. With each passing year the distance between these two poles grew shorter; and when I found my way to the Sarvodaya Movement in Sri Lanka, the two paths seemed to converge.

After my initial encounter with A.T. Ariyaratna, the founder and president of Sarvodaya, he invited me to come back and study the role of religion in this Buddhist-inspired self-help movement. It was with a sense of "coming home" that I greeted that opportunity, and when the Ford Foundation offered funds for expenses, I undertook this study in the field from June 1979 to June 1980.

Let me emphasize that the object of my purpose was not to evaluate the Sarvodaya Movement, whether in terms of its economic or educational impact, nor was it to measure the strengths and weaknesses of its structures, policies, and programs. Other studies, referred to in the text and listed in the bibliography, attempt this. While all such assessments attest to the grassroots vitality of the Movement, which engages the energies of people in over four thousand villages, none, understandably enough, undertakes to examine the sources of this vitality—nor to seek them in indigenous religious tradition as it has been evoked, revitalized, and reinterpreted by Sarvodaya leaders. It is that which I set out to do.

I went in order to learn how religious beliefs and aspirations are reflected in the goals of the Movement and how they serve to engage the people's trust and energy. I wanted to see and hear how they are conveyed and put to work through language, behavior and organizing techniques.

To do this, I focused primarily on the grassroots level. I settled in a village near a regional Sarvodaya District Center and traveled widely to over thirty other villages as well as to Sarvodaya's national headquarters in Moratuwa. I observed local organizers at work and villagers of all ages and backgrounds as they participated in Sarvodaya activities. In addition to interviewing the Movement's top-level leadership and many members of the headquarter's personnel, I interviewed over a hundred Sarvodayan monks, lay organizers, and village participants. I also interviewed more than thirty local government personnel and extension agents engaged in related activities. I observed non-Sarvodaya projects as well, both public and private, and interviewed villagers and local leaders external to the Movement. To deepen my understanding of the Movement, I participated in its activities, attending some hundred or so meetings and "family gatherings" and engaging in manual labor at a dozen *shramadana* work camps. I became for two weeks a trainee—the first Westerner, to my knowledge, to go through the Sarvodaya training program for women preparing to return to their villages as preschool teachers and community organizers. While "on the road" from my village home, I was accorded hospitality by many families both within and outside the Sarvodaya Movement. In addition to enjoying their company, I learned a great deal from them about the present pressures of Sri Lankan life and about Sarvodaya.

My knowledge of the Sinhalese language was adequate for casual conversation; for interviews and most meetings I engaged interpreters. A motorcycle permitted me access to the remotest of villages and work projects. My background as a scholar of Buddhism and my status as a practicing Buddhist, as well as my "elderly" age (at fifty), helped me gain the confidence of lay people and clergy alike. Earlier visitors had generally been younger people and of different religious faiths, which is why—as villagers often stated—they had not expressed themselves so freely with a foreigner before. Monks were surprised and pleased to learn that the woman steering the motorcycle up the dirt road to their temple was, in America, likewise a teacher of the Dharma; and they were ready to discuss the philosophical as well as the practical aspects of their community work. Their welcome also facilitated the trust and openness of the many village people who enriched my work and life in Sri Lanka.

What I learned surprised me. Familiar with Sarvodaya slogans and speeches, I knew that religion—or the Dharma—played a role in legitimizing the Movement and supplying its leaders with inspirational rhetoric. What I did *not* expect was to find that it permeates the Movement at every level, shaping not only its goals but its tactics, not only at Headquarters but in the village, not only among monks and temple devotees but among tenant farmers and school dropouts. I have tried, therefore, where space permits, to include their own words.

In offering this little book, I am happy to tender my thanks to those who made it possible. To "Ari", first and foremost, goes my gratitude for his example, his openness, and his trust in urging me to "go see for yourself" (*ehi passiko*). That appreciation extends to all his co-workers in the Sarvodaya family who opened their doors and minds to Joanna-akka. They are too numerous to name, but I would offer special thanks to my brothers "Jothi" Dassanayaka of the Baddegama center and "Hewa" Hewavitharana of the Matara center for helping me enter the world of village Sri Lanka.

For believing in the value of this research and supporting it financially, I am grateful to the Ford Foundation and thank Adrienne Germaine, Eugene Staples, and Dr. Kamla Chowdhry for their trust and challenge. For believing in *me* and supporting me emotionally, I honor my husband and children. Thank you, Fran, Peggy, Jack, and Chris, for holding me close across the miles and then coming to share my Sri Lankan world. For help in preparing this manuscript I thank my colleague, Kathy Knight.

In these acknowledgements I have saved my *bhikku* friends till last. It is these monks, most of all, who symbolize for me the convergence of Dharma and development. In their company—sitting and talking in a cool temple compound or walking a hot, dusty road to a work project—I beheld their intellect and courage, and felt the two halves of my life come together. As one does not thank a monk, I shall simply mention Ven. G. Saranankara, Ven. T. Sumanatissa, Ven. K. Pannasagara, Ven. G. Uditha, Ven. U. Sarana, and the late Ven. H. Gnanaseeha, to name but a few of those Sarvodayan monks whose work among the oppressed gave me insight into the possibilities of the human spirit. *Pin siddha veccawe* (may your merit increase)!

Any merit accruing from my writing and dissemination of this book is transferred to all fellow-beings. May all creatures be happy!

JOANNA MACY
Washington, D.C. 1982

Preface to the Revised Edition

In 1984 I returned for two extensive visits to the Sarvodaya Shramadana Movement. The time that had elapsed since my year of field work in Sri Lanka had altered the climate in which the Movement works and also, to a lesser extent, its internal operations.

The ethnic conflict between Sinhalese and Tamils had spread, grown more severe, erupted in largescale violence. Earlier it had been a subject of concern, now it was—and is—a dominant and often devastating feature of life for present-day Sri Lankans. Even for the bulk of the population whose daily pursuits are undisturbed, its shadow across their hearts and minds obsesses them as much as a civil war. I was eager to know how this conflict affected the Movement, and how Sarvodayans were working within a context of growing polarization.

Also, during this time, Sarvodaya had altered its internal structure. In 1980 I had seen it concocting plans to decentralize—plans which represented the Movement's longterm intention to create local autonomous structures. This intention was consonant with the Buddha's teachings, on which Sarvodaya based both its goals and methods. And I wanted to know whether and how Sarvodaya had managed an internal redistribution of power during a period of such national turbulence.

This expanded edition of *Dharma and Development* includes, in Chapter Nine, a report on these two developments.

As in my earlier study, I approached the Movement with the desire to understand the values which guide its work and which it elicits in mobilizing popular participation. Then, as before, it was not my purpose to evaluate the Movement in terms of its effectiveness in economic or community development. Rather I sought to understand how traditional indigenous value systems—and in particular the Buddha Dharma—serve to help Sarvodayans define what development *is,* and how they served to mobilize people to work together. In a world where people are increasingly alienated from, and simultaneously hungry for abiding values by which to guide their social, economic, political and military interactions, this seems a worthy object of study.

In this regard, it was as instructive to see what had *not* changed in Sarvodaya, as it was to see what had. After over three years away from the Movement on its home turf, I was again struck, almost surprised, by the extent to which Sarvodayans at all levels articulated the purposes of their activities in terms of "awakening," and in terms of the compassion, self-reliance and nonpartisanship that this awakening represents to them. And I was struck again that Sarvodaya means to them the "awakening of *all,*" Tamils as well as Sinhalese, merchants as well as laborers, civil servants as well as malnourished children. The Sarvodayan goals and methods described in this book still hold. This edition does not correct so much as expand, reflecting in its last chapter the chief issues facing the Movement in the mid-80's and the response that it makes to them, out of the assumptions it derives from the Dharma.

JOANNA MACY
Sausalito 1985

Introduction

Sarvodaya signifies the awakening or liberation of *one and all*, without exception, *Sabbe satta sukhi hontu*, "May all beings be well and happy," is the Buddhist wish, in contrast to the Hegelian concept of the welfare of the majority. In a world where greed, hatred, and ignorance are so well organized, is it possible for this thought of the well-being of all to be effectively practiced for the regeneration of man and society? The answer to that question lies in the lives of hundreds of thousands of village people in Sri Lanka who have embraced the Sarvodaya way to development. For Sarvodaya, since 1958, has grown from a small group of young pioneers, working alongside the outcaste poor, to a people's self-help movement that is presently active in over four thousand towns and villages, operating programs for health, education, agriculture, and local industry.

The Sarvodaya Movement has been able to attain such scope and vitality because it has not tried to apply any ready-made solutions or development schemes from above; instead it has gone to the people to draw forth the strength and intelligence that are innate in them and that are encouraged by their age-old traditions.

Some development experts would argue that in our fast-changing world, preparing briskly for industrialization and modernization, tradition has no meaningful role to perform; but the initiators of Sarvodaya believe that without the understanding of tradition no new theory or program forced on the people, however ingenious it may be, will reap the desired results. No program will be effective, further-more, that tries to separate the economic aspect of life from the cultural and spiritual aspects, as do both the capitalist and socialist models of development, with their sole emphasis on the production of goods and their neglect of the full range of human well-being. For his well-being the needs of the whole person must be met, needs that include satisfying work, harmonious relationships, a safe and beautiful environment, and a life of the mind and spirit, as well as food, clothing, and shelter.

To meet these needs Sarvodaya has committed itself to a dynamic non-violent revolution which is not a transfer of political, economic, or social power from one party or class to another, but the transfer of all such power to the people. For that purpose man as well as society must change. The person himself must awaken to his true needs and true strengths if the society is to prosper without conflict and injustice. From the wisdom embodied in our religious traditions we can cull principles for that kind of personal and collective awakening. That is what Sarvodaya has done—listening to the villagers, who constitute eighty percent of our country, and articulating a challenge in terms of the ideals they still revere and in words that make sense to them.

Any understanding of Sarvodaya is therefore incomplete if it does not sufficiently recognize the resources that our Movement has drawn from the spiritual and cultural traditions of our people. That is why I am happy that Dr. Joanna Macy has written this book, for it shows these resources quite clearly, together with the central role they play in our theory and practice.

Dr. Macy is well suited to offer such a perspective on our work. She is not only acquainted with problems of the Third World, having spent years in development efforts in South Asia and Africa, but she is also a serious student of religion, deeply informed by the study and practice of Buddhism. During her recent year with Sarvodaya she lived side by side with the villagers and gained their trust by her readiness to work and her reverent understanding of their religious beliefs. Unlike many Western scholars who overemphasize that aspect of Buddhism which preaches the renunciation of worldly life, she is well aware of the social teachings of the Lord Buddha and was in a position to recognize them in the workings of Sarvodaya. In the Buddha's teachings as much emphasis is given to community awakening and community organizational factors as to the awakening of the individual. This fact was unfortunately lost from view during the long colonial period when Western powers attempted to weaken the influence of the Sangha (the Order of Monks) and to separate the subjugated people from the inspiration to dignity, power, and freedom which they could find in their tradition.

Let us be clear, however, that when we speak of tradition and its role in development, we do not limit our understanding to Buddhism. The example and relevance of Sarvodaya would be very restricted if we thought it only has meaning for Buddhist societies. As Dr. Macy points out, the Sarvodaya Movement, while originally inspired by the Buddhist tradition, is active throughout our multi-ethnic society, working with Hindu, Muslim, and Christian communities and involving scores of thousands of Hindu, Muslim, and Christian co-workers. Our message of awakening transcends any effort to categorize it as the teaching of a particular creed. Through the philosophy of Sarvodaya—based on loving-kindness, compassionate action, altruistic joy and equanimity, as well as on sharing, pleasant speech, constructive work, and equality—people of different faiths and ethnic origins are motivated to carve out a way of life and a path of development founded on these ideals.

Because these ideals are universal, Sarvodaya has been able to bring harmony into situations of ethnic and religious conflict that exist here in Sri Lanka, and to play a unique role in allaying hostility by enlisting people in common projects. For the same reasons the experience of Sarvodaya can have meaning for the rest of the world in these troubled times. The suffering of humanity today is not limited to the countries that are called underdeveloped, nor to the more dramatic cases of hunger, disease, and stagnation. It extends to citizens of the industrialized nations as well, where millions are held in the grip of fear and powerlessness as they face unemployment, inflation, the arms race, and mounting conflict. There, too, can be tapped the spiritual traditions of humanity, be they Christian, Jewish, Muslim, or native American; they can challenge and help people to act with non-violence, compassion, and discipline. There, too, can be heard the message of awakening—the *vishvodaya* or world-awakening which is the ultimate goal of our Movement.

A. T. ARIYARATNA
President
Sarvodaya Shramadana Movement

I

"Temple and Tank": The Relevance of Religion to Development

Ancient Ceylon, in the centuries before the colonial powers came, was known as the Land of Plenty and the Isle of Righteousness. Beside the vast network of irrigation canals and reservoirs (or tanks) that made the island the "Granary of the East," rose great temples and stupas of the Buddhist order. These sacred edifices were constructed from the earth excavated for the canals and tanks, whose construction and maintenance were supervised by the monks. That history lives today in the minds of those Sri Lankans who speak of the inherent relationship between "temple and tank," or between religion and development.

WHAT HAS RELIGION TO DO WITH DEVELOPMENT? TO MOST planners and administrators who designed programs in the 1960s and '70s to alleviate conditions of poverty in "underdeveloped" or "lesser-developed" countries, the religious traditions of a given society were considered peripheral. Ancient indigenous belief systems and practices were, by and large, viewed as hangovers from a pre-colonial past which had little relevance for social and economic modernization. They were even seen as obstacles to overcome in freeing people from apparent superstition and passivity, and in transferring the technology that would bring them unencumbered into the workplace and market of the twentieth century.

The transfer of technology turned out, as we know, to be not so simple a process. Often it boomeranged, exacerbating local inequities, creating patterns of dependence, and leaving behind, along with rusting unused equipment, an increased sense of frustration and powerlessness.

Grappling with these problems, development planners and

scholars have in the last years broadened the discussion of world development issues to embrace two significant concerns. One is the importance of popular participation, i.e., the necessity of involving local communities, not as targets so much as actors in a development process aimed at meeting basic human needs. The other is the consideration of underlying value-systems; for development is no longer seen as value-free, nor its efficacy as independent of the ethical norms and traditions of a given culture.

It is in the light of both of these concerns, each of which presents a major challenge to our customary ways of thinking about world development, that the role of religion becomes apparent. Before considering its relevance to each of these issues, let us clarify our use of the term *religion*.

THE MEANING OF *RELIGION*

As in the academic study of religious traditions, we use the term *religion* to mean more than its institutional forms in ecclesiastical structures, personnel, rituals, and creeds. The concept extends beyond these outer forms to include what they represent—an integrated set of values, or the core principles perceived to be at the root of phenomenal reality and at the heart of human fulfillment. These unquestioned values, transcending all others, provide the context within which life's purposes and activities are found meaningful and good. This, in Buddhist culture, is close to the concept of Dharma. The term means both the teachings of the Buddha and the central content of these teachings, which is the law of reality or the way life works.

The word religion comes from *religare*, to bind together. Envisioning the ultimate nature and purpose of existence, it gives order to the buzzing confusion of sensory life and lets interlinking patterns of meaning emerge. Thus it serves as the *context of meaning* in which values are perceived and human choices are made.

A religious system also provides the means by which these values are appropriated—through precepts, stories, myths, collective rituals, and personal practices. Religion is method as well as vision. It serves as both model and structure for transformation. Whether the goal of transformation be seen as salvation, liberation, the kingdom of God, or the awakening of all, procedures designed to effect it are, by nature, religious.

Religion in its institutional forms has not always played a transformational role, of course; it has often been used to obstruct social change and bolster the status quo. In every religious tradition instances abound where ecclesiastical organization, its possessions and prestige, have played a politically reactionary role, helping to legitimate and extend the autocratic use of power. But over and over, because it is ultimately rooted in a transcendent vision of human fulfillment, religion breaks through habitual social and conceptual structures to inspire their renewal and change. As can be seen in every tradition, from Gandhi's work within Hinduism to the worker priests of the Roman Catholic church, religion can provide the dynamism for reformist and even revolutionary activity, as it taps its own roots to rearticulate the possibilities of the human spirit.

RELIGION AND DEVELOPMENT VALUES

The problems of world development are essentially problems of priority. They are a function of the values that operate in the perception and determination of needs and in the production and distribution of wealth. The crises we face—in growing economic disparities, the struggle for resources, destruction of the biosphere, the arms race—arise from human decisions; they reflect assumptions and goals that are, at root, of an ethical nature.

Many of our current assumptions and goals have been shaped in industrial societies based on competition and unchecked exploitation of material resources. Although they once seemed appropriate to economic well-being, their viability in a crowded, interdependent, and ecologically vulnerable world is now being questioned. It is increasingly recognized that efforts to apply technological, monetary, and administrative "fixes," while remaining within the value-system of the old industrial system, only compound our problems— and that a reassessment of the values themselves is in order. That is fitting, for all remedies and strategies find their source in notions of what is good and who is valuable. As economist Hazel Henderson asserts,

> "Value-systems and ethics, far from being peripheral, are the dominant, driving variables in all economic and technological systems".[1]

The consideration of ethical norms and moral value brings us willy-nilly into the domain of religion, representing, as it does, our ultimate assessment of what is real and what is worthwhile. To the extent that Marxism, national socialism, or capitalism claims to embody the *summum bonum*, the final perception and fulfillment of life, they too are religious; where they are understood to serve more limited means and are judged by broader or higher standards, these very standards are religious in nature. Of this nature are the final criteria operative in the allocation of resources, time, energy. Whether or not these criteria *appear* religious, they stem from value-systems—or

---

[1] Hazel Henderson, speech at *World Future Society*, Toronto, 1980.

are re-ordered in the light of value-systems—which, in the last analysis, are articles of faith.

RELIGION AND POPULAR PARTICIPATION IN DEVELOPMENT

Development efforts over the last two and a half decades have demonstrated that, however clever or generous the schemes, the local populace will not use them or profit from them unless it is internally motivated to do so. Nor will the intended beneficiaries of any plan carry it out unless it makes sense to them, meeting their needs as *they* see such needs. Their energies, allegiance, and values must be enlisted if programs are to take root and sustain themselves on a continuing basis.

Here again we encounter the question of values. To enlist popular participation and commitment, development programs require a value-base that is meaningful to the people, relevant to their perceived needs, and affirmative of their inherent strengths.

And where are such values to be found? They are present in indigenous religious traditions, which over the centuries have shaped the people's perception of reality and their notions of what is good and true. Principles for the improvement of their present lives can be culled from these traditions—and re-articulated in ways that mobilize people to take responsibility for social change. This is the experience of a variety of grassroots movements around the world, from Gandhigram in India to "basismo" communities in Brazil, in which traditional religious teachings are recast so as to release human energy for community action. This is also the experience of the Sarvodaya Shramadana Movement in Sri Lanka.

As a people's self-help movement, which grew from a handful of young volunteers to be Sri Lanka's largest non-governmental organization with activities in over four thousand villages, Sarvodaya serves as a dramatic and instructive example of the relevance of tradition to development; for it bases both its theory and its practice on a clearly articulated value-system drawn from its culture's religious heritage.

In Sri Lanka that heritage is primarily Buddhist, since over seventy percent of the population adhere to the Buddhist path, also known as the Buddha-dharma, or simply the Dharma. While the Sarvodaya Movement includes many Hindus, Muslims, and Christians, it is preeminently the teachings of the Buddha on which it bases its philosophy of development—and those principles of personal and collective awakening that it now finds and summons in other faith-systems as well.

II

The Sarvodaya Shramadana Movement

A LUNGI-CLAD YOUNG WOMAN GREETING HER FRIENDS AS SHE returns on foot, with her valise, to a remote village . . . families assembling and weaving palm fronds to thatch a roof for a preschool . . . toddlers learning songs, getting vaccinated, bringing matchboxes of rice to share . . . mothers preparing food in a community kitchen, starting a sewing class, pooling rupees for a machine . . . a procession of villagers with picks and banners heading out to cut a road through the jungle . . . a monk in orange robes calling on government officials in their file-filled offices, inviting them to join the group, and to supply the cement for culverts . . . police cadets in the city coming to training courses on community awakening . . . prisoners released from jail to work with neighborhood families to clear parks and playgrounds for their children . . . school dropouts organizing masonry workshops in a corner of a temple compound . . . monks and laypeople chanting sacred verses as a new community shop is opened, as a mile of irrigation canal is dredged of weeds, as a hand-built windmill is erected and begins to pump . . . while in the temple's preaching hall villagers gather to hear their children sing ancient songs and to discuss the construction of community latrines.

What can such a multiplicity of scenes and actors have in common? Each is a fragment of the larger whole that is Sarvodaya. What weaves that whole together, basic to all the purposes and activities of the Movement, is a philosophy of development based on indigenous religious tradition, that is, on the Dharma. Before examining how it works, let us look briefly at the larger scene in which these actors move.

CONTEXT

The island republic of Sri Lanka, or Ceylon as it used to be called, hangs like a tear off the Southeastern coast of India—a tear almost the size of Ireland, with a population of some 14.5 million people. This "pearl of the Indian ocean" was also called, in ancient times before the Western colonizers came, the "Isle of Righteousness" and the "Granary of the East"; but now, though still beautiful, it is ravaged by the poverty endemic to most pre-industrial, post-colonial countries.

It presents many features typical of such countries. After four centuries under the rule of the Portuguese, the Dutch, and then the British, it found itself, when it regained independence in 1948, with a plantation economy (largely tea, rubber, and coconut) dependent on exports and vulnerable to the vagaries of international trade. With exports of commodity cash crops amounting to 70% of her GNP, Sri Lanka's economic position became increasingly precarious as the terms of trade moved against her and as successive governments attempted to meet internal needs through massive welfare programs in health, education, and food subsidies. By the 1950s the largely rural population (over 80% of the country) had begun to sink into economic stagnation with all the consequent apathy, sense of powerlessness, and isolation. As if in mockery of its ancient identity as Dhanagana, "land of plenty", it became one of the poorest countries in the world, with an annual per-capita income of $130.

In two distinctive ways, however, Sri Lanka presents a contrast to other poor countries. First, it is unique in the progress it has made in stemming the birth rate, extending life expectancy, and increasing literacy. These factors, rated in the Physical Quality of Life Index as devised by the Overseas Development Council, show Sri Lanka to enjoy a higher quality of life than countries with even ten times the per-capita income. Moreover, while the gap between rich and poor within most societies has widened, in Sri Lanka, until the last few years, it narrowed. Figures comparing 1953 and 1970 reflect a redistribution of income between the highest and lowest quintiles of the population.[1]

Secondly, it is noteworthy that these achievements were made within a democratic, multi-party system. Having won universal suffrage as early as 1931, Sri Lanka is both one of the oldest and one of the few remaining democracies in the Third World. Its relatively educated population is proud and protective of its participation in political life.

Given the make-up of the population, this self-governance is not without some profound tensions. As Goulet puts it,[2] two polarities pull at the body politic. One is between the Westernized, English-speaking, largely urban elite and the Sinhalese-speaking rural masses—the

---

[1] Lester Brown, *The Twenty-ninth Day* (W.W. Norton, New York: 1978), Chapter 9.

[2] Denis Goulet, *Survival with Integrity* (Colombo: Marga Institute, 1981), p. 28.

Sinhalese ethnic group constituting 70% of the population. This tension fed into the bloody, Marxist-led uprising of 1971, which is called the Insurgency, and in which many young people now working nonviolently with Sarvodaya took part.

The second polarity, which is at present more sorely felt, is that between the Sinhalese themselves and the Tamils. The Tamils, who are Hindu and derive originally from Southern India, comprise two groups: the Ceylonese Tamils (11% of the population) who settled in Northern Ceylon many centuries ago and achieved considerable educational and administrative power under colonial rule, and the "estate" Tamils (7%) who were brought over within recent generations to labor on British tea estates. It is among the more educated Ceylonese Tamils, living mainly in the area of the Jaffna peninsula, that resentments against discrimination by the Sinhalese Buddhist majority are felt and fought. These resentments, centering around language (the use of Sinhalese as official tongue) and restricted access to university education and government posts, have fomented ill will on both sides. On occasion this has erupted in violent civic strife and impositions of martial law.

Also to be noted as part of the backdrop to the Sarvodaya Movement, are the development policies of the current party in power. Elected in 1977, the right-of-center United National Party turned from the socialist-oriented practices of the previous government to move toward the Western model of free enterprise. While reluctant to cut back on the bulk of social services, which would be politically hazardous, the UNP has sought to foster growth and employment by (1) developing export-oriented manufacturing through free-trade zones, called Investment Promotion Zones, and dropping restrictions on imports; (2) undertaking massive capital-intensive, foreign-financed development schemes in construction and irrigation, such as the ambitious and controversial Accelerated Mahaweli (River) Program; and (3) the promotion of international tourism, with the expansion of high-cost resort areas, as a means of earning foreign currency. These policies, are invigorating to large-scale private enterprise, but they erode village industry and are powerless to stem spiraling inflation; as a consequence they foster a dual economy, exacerbating the gap between the poor, rural sectors of the population and the urban elite.

It is a testimony to the present Sri Lankan government's commitment to economic and political pluralism that it can not only tolerate but encourages and cooperates with the Sarvodaya Movement; for Sarvodaya pursues an alternate path of development, as we shall see in the next chapter. Being Sri Lanka's largest non-governmental organization, involving an estimated two to three million people in its varied programs, its potential impact on the country is considerable.

SARVODAYA HISTORY

Sarvodaya leaders stress repeatedly that, while their theory of development is distinctive, it did not precede but rather emerged from the Movement's experience in village self-help. Rather than a blueprint produced by academic research, theory followed action and is still evolving.[3] What then is the story of this generative experience?

It began in 1958 with a group of 16- and 17-year-old students from Nalanda College, the prestigious Buddhist high school which had been founded in Colombo at the turn of the century by the American theosophist Col. Henry Olcott, and which was noted for its excellent cricket teams. The students' young science teacher, A.T. Ariyaratna, inspired and helped them to organize a two-week "holiday work camp" in a remote and destitute outcaste village. Ariyaratna wanted his students

> to understand and experience the true state of affairs that prevailed in the rural and poor urban areas. . .(and) to develop a love for their people and utilize the education they received to find ways of building a more just and happier life for them.[4]

From the outset they went to learn what the villagers themselves needed and wanted, living in their huts, sharing their diet, working side by side sinking wells and planting gardens, and talking till late at night in village "family gatherings." They called the camp *shramadana*, from *dana* (to give) and *shrama* (labor or human energy). The experience was so rewarding that the shramadana idea caught on and spread. Within a couple of years hundreds of schools joined in the practice of giving labor at weekend village camps, and a national Shramadana Movement was under way.

As the students graduated and took leadership as adults, and as monks and others joined them, the Movement fanned out beyond the school system, expanding its focus from an educational effort to a developmental one, where the villagers themselves took the initiative. The Shramadana Movement began to emerge as a village self-help movement outside the official rural development program. Meanwhile Ariyaratna went to India to learn from the Gandhian experience and particularly from the Bhoodan-Gramdan campaign led by the walking scholar-saint Vinoba Bhave. Since Gandhian ideals echoed his own, Ariyaratna brought back the term that Gandhi had used for the ideal society based on truth, nonviolence, and self-reliance; and he named his plan the Sarvodaya Shramadana Movement.

---

[3]A.T. Ariyaratna, *In Search of Development* (Moratuwa: Sarvodaya Press, 1981), p. 1.
[4]*Ibid.* p. 3.

In 1968 Ariyaratna took the bold step of testing the validity of his approach and the dedication of his young colleagues by initiating the Hundred Villages Development Scheme in some of the most impoverished of Sri Lanka's 23,000 villages. Capital resources were virtually non-existent, but with help from Dutch and German donors the program took hold, elaborating and refining its methods of community awakening. This Hundred Villages Scheme, which seemed wildly ambitious at the outset, spread within ten years to two thousand villages; in the following three years it had reached over four thousand.

During the 1970s, with the help from foreign agencies as well many Sri Lankan well-wishers, Sarvodaya had established a headquarters and main training center in Moratuwa, near Colombo, and a dozen regional centers where community organizers and extension workers in health, preschool education, agriculture, cottage industry, and village technology were also trained. It has organized over a hundred Gramodaya ("village awakening") Centers, each designed to service and coordinate programs in twenty to thirty nearby villages. It was on this base that by 1980 the Movement entered a new stage, one which Ariyaratna sees as moving beyond purely "developmental" activities to "structural change."[5]

Putting to the test its belief in local self-reliance, the Movement undertook a radical and methodical decentralization of power, giving to local centers decision-making responsibilities in program and budget. In this deliberate relinquishment of central control, which is a rare phenomenon indeed, hundreds of Village Awakening Councils or *Samhitis* have been legally incorporated. Empowered to develop, conduct, and coordinate their own developmental programs, these councils are constituted to include balanced numbers of children, women, and youths as well as men and village elders. Further structural changes have included: (1) granting autonomy to major spin-offs of the Movement, such as the Sarvodaya Research Institute, the Bhikkus (Monks) Program, and Suwa Setha, the homes for abandoned and handicapped children; (2) creating locally administered community shops to increase competition and to lower prices of goods available to villagers; and (3) establishing a Deshodaya (National Awakening) Council to spur nonpartisan discussion of national policies and opportunities.

SARVODAYA PROGRAM

How does Sarvodaya structure its developmental activities? To understand its organization we will proceed, as Sarvodaya organizers

---

[5]*Ibid.* pp. 1 ff.

do, "from the bottom up." But it should also be kept in mind that, given the wide variety in local conditions, the vagaries of human nature, the deficiencies of funds, and the Movement's reluctance to impose any schema "from above," the following sketch, while descriptive of some villages, represents an idealized picture when applied to the Movement as a whole. The sketch is a composite; many villages in which Sarvodaya works do not include the full range of the activities it describes.

The process begins when a village invites a Sarvodaya worker to initiate a program of activity. Note that since the demand for the Movement's help far exceeds the supply, it rarely enters the scene unsolicited. As a first step, this worker checks in with the local monk and other key figures, and prompts them to assemble a *paule hamua* or "family gathering" of local inhabitants, sometimes in the school, but usually in the temple or preaching hall. Here the initial Sarvodaya "pitch" or message is given, telling about the awakening that is happening elsewhere in the country and inviting the villagers to begin to take charge of their own lives by discussing frankly together their common needs. To focus their discussion, the organizer challenges the villagers to undertake a *shramadana* or shared labor project in which they take responsibility for identifying, agreeing upon, and meeting a specific need. This could be cutting an access road, cleaning a well, digging latrines, etc. A work camp is then organized and in the process of its organization, which takes a month or two and involves many villagers, local task forces are formed. Either before or during that first shramadana camp, which can last from a day to several weeks but is usually a weekend, embryonic Sarvodaya "groups" coalesce: the youth group and mothers' group usually form first, with the children's group and farmers' and elders' groups coming later. Sometimes this process is initiated by a Sarvodaya-trained preschool teacher, but in any case a shramadana constitutes the usual initial organizing mechanism.

With the organizing of on-going groups through a shramadana, the village now enters a second stage where the groups identify their own priorities and initiate their own program, such as planting a garden or conducting a house-to-house survey. The Movement supplies ideas, contacts, skills, and even credit and materials through its Gramodaya Centers (next level up) and its regional and national facilities. Young people who have demonstrated particular motivation and effectiveness are chosen by their groups to undertake training at the nearest Sarvodaya Institute. This training may be in community organizing or in health and preschool education or in a given technical skill (agriculture, batik, metal-working, bookkeeping, etc., depending on what projects are locally appropriate and feasible). It is more likely to be put into use, when the trainees return with their acquired skills, because they are of the village and have been locally selected by their peers. This process, which beginning with the shramadana is open to all, permits the emergence of local leadership that is an alternative to the power customarily exerted by the larger landowners and merchants.

As local efforts take root, the Movement's national and regional network has yet other resources to offer, such as practical skills in organizing local marketing cooperatives and saving schemes, in monitoring the incidence of malnutrition and disease, and in creating locally appropriate rural technology. These resources also include legal aid services, library services, the development of community shops, immunization and nutritional programs in conjunction with state and international agencies, and Shanti Sena ("peace-keeping army") leagues where volunteers are trained in crowd control, emergency first aid, and conflict resolution. When a village has reached the point where its children's, youth, mothers', farmers', and elders' groups are functional, it is ready to incorporate its own Village Awakening Council, which then serves as an autonomous legal entity designing its own developmental program.

In guiding this development, the Sarvodaya Movement relies on its identification of the Ten Basic Needs. Considered essential to human well-being, these are: water, food, housing, clothing, health care, communication, fuel, education, a clean, safe, beautiful environment, and a spiritual and cultural life. This list serves both to guide village projects, giving equal priority to some factors which appear "non-economic," and to help Sarvodayans set their other wants into perspective. In the light of these fundamental requirements for a decent and worthy life, all other wants appear as motivated by greed, sloth, or ignorance.

Sarvodaya, furthermore—which means "the awakening of all"—sets its program within the context of four kinds of awakening: personal awakening, village awakening, national awakening, and world awakening. The first two are evident in the programs described above; their dynamics are examined in this book. National awakening, which is implicit in them, also takes the form of a Deshodaya Council, a sort of country-wide "council of elders" where chief actors and analysts step back to look, in nonpartisan discussions, at the drift and challenge of events.

For world awakening (vishvodaya) the Movement's actions include the following:

1. It receives foreign visitors and volunteers who come to observe

and participate in the Sarvodaya program, and offers them orientation and a measure of logistical support. About three hundred came in the last year, with over a hundred (mostly German, Dutch, and Danish) staying for over a month and some (including the eighteen mostly Asian young people with the United Nations Volunteer program) remaining to work and learn for a year or two.

2. It offers technical assistance to other Third World countries. In addition to training foreign teams (such as Central African village workers or a deputation of Thai monks), it provides Sarvodayan organizers to go back and work with them, as in the project now underway in Mali.

3. After convening international conferences in Sri Lanka in 1978 and in Holland in 1981, it incorporated Sarvodaya International, a world-wide organization interlinking groups and individuals— from the industrialized North as well as the developing South— who subscribe to the Sarvodaya philosophy and who connect to coordinate actions for mutual support.

4. In addition to its local publications in Sinhalese and Tamil, it offers to a wider audience an English-language journal (*Dana*) and writings, reports, tapes, and films descriptive of the Movement's philosophy and work. Within a larger context, this book itself would be viewed as both means and evidence of "world awakening."

So vast an undertaking would not, of course, be possible without outside help. The ideas, vigor, and experience of Ariyaratna and his co-workers would have benefitted far fewer people—and be known by few beyond Sri Lankan shores—had not sympathetic donors provided funds for training, construction, transport, and program. Protective of his movement's autonomy and reluctant to receive aid from his own or any other government, Ariyaratna has accepted donations to Sarvodaya from private or semi-private foreign agencies (chiefly Dutch, German, and, more recently, American) and these have come to amount to over eighty percent of the Movement's monetary budget. So high a percentage of foreign aid has brought criticism to the Movement, and raised the question of how seriously it takes its own goal of self-help. In the next chapter, in the section on self-reliance, we will see how Ariyaratna replies to such criticism, setting the issue within the context of global inequalities and of the uncomputed gifts of time, labor, and skills which the Movement generates.

Meanwhile we may note that the Movement is phenomenally successful in mobilizing people on the village level, and that this grass-roots vitality is something no foreign money can buy and no government program can confer. According to Ariyaratna, the Movement engages about a hundred thousand full-time workers, only six percent of whom receive a living allowance. And this allowance, it should be noted, amounts to some five to fifteen dollars a month. Clearly Sarvodaya does not buy its way into the lives of its people; many engage in the Movement at considerable personal cost, working long hours with no pay. The chief rewards, obviously, are non-monetary. What then are they? How are the goals and means of development so presented and so lived that they motivate these people to give time and energy in so abundant a manner?

It is the thesis of this book that the roots of this commitment are to be found in religion. Because for Sri Lanka this religion is predominantly Buddhism, we refer to the Dharma. Yet in doing so, let us emphasize that Sarvodaya, like Sri Lanka, is religiously plural and grounds its work in other faith systems as well.

RELIGIOUS PLURALISM IN SARVODAYA

Because the Movement's "philosophy"[6] is predominantly expressed in Buddhist terms—in its literature, language, ceremony and even Headquarters architecture[7]—it is easy to assume that religion in Sarvodaya means Buddhism. Such an equation is inaccurate, for other faith systems play a role in Sarvodaya too— both in the ideals and strategies which inspired the Movement's birth and in its current activities in Christian, Hindu, and Muslim communities.

The first shramadanas organized in 1958 and 1959 were in substantial measure inspired by the youth work camps organized in post-war Europe by Quakers and other church groups. First-hand accounts of them were brought back to Sri Lanka by D.A. Abeysekere, a Rural Development official and close friend of Ariyaratna, who worked with him to design the initial "holiday work camps" at Kanatholuwa and Manawa. It was these camps that launched the movement of Sarvodaya.

In formulating its philosophy and goals, the Movement took inspiration from the Gandhians, as the name it adopted attests. It gave, however, a new set of meaning to Gandhi's concept. Ideas to be effective must merge with the indigenous ethos and interact with the specific genius of a culture. Gandhi himself knew this when he took the inspiration he found in the Sermon on the Mount to reinterpret the *Bhagavad Gita* and tap the potentials of his own Hindu tradition. Ariyaratna knew this in taking the Gandhian vision, experienced first-hand with Vinoba Bhave, and recasting it in new and fruitful ways within the belief structure of Sinhalese Buddhism. What emerged is a philosophy-in-

[6]"Philosophy" (*darshana*) is the term Sarvodayans use for the Movement's ideology—its goals for personal and social change and the moral assumptions which underly them.

[7]The headquarters building in Moratuwa is called "Damsak Mandir" (Wheel of

action which is culturally specific to Sri Lanka, yet international in its appeal—and also in its applicability, through the ongoing processes of cross-cultural adaptation.

That the Movement's religious identification is not exclusively Buddhist is evident in its activities among other religious communities, in its inclusion of Christian, Hindu, and Muslim symbols and rituals (their prayers are usually placed first in the "family gatherings" where religious minorities are present), in its utilization of churches, mosques, and kovils (Hindu temples) for its operations (frequently organizing work camps to clean and repair them), in the work of Hindu and Christian priests and Muslim imams in its local programs, and in the ways in which its goals of nonviolence, self-reliance, economic sharing, and social equality are articulated in the thought-forms of these other religions. It is clear that the Movement not only embraces non-Buddhists but also can relate to them in the actual terms of their own religious symbol-systems. Yet, because Sarvodaya is predominantly Buddhist both in its membership (there is a higher proportion of Buddhists in Sarvodaya than in the country) and in public expressions of its philosophy, I will refer to the Dharma—i.e., to Buddhist concepts and practices—in reflecting on the role of religion in Sarvodaya.

Dharma) and is constructed on an open octagonal plan. Each section around the central courtyard represents one aspect of the Eight-fold Path: for example, the hostel for volunteers is in Right Action and the accounting office in Right Mindfulness.

III

Religion and the Goals of Development

I N THE SARVODAYA MOVEMENT RELIGION SERVES AS A RESOURCE, not in order to rationalize the need for development programs or to attract the traditional and pious elements of society, so much as to shape the ends and means of development itself. Religious assumptions and values serve to define the very nature of development and, in so doing, to frame the goals and practices of the organization. These goals and practices, furthermore, are not just preached by the leaders of the Movement; as I found from experience in over thirty villages, they are discussed among people at the grassroots level as they engage in Sarvodaya activities.

Their comments and their actions in sharing responsibility for these activities indicated that goals derived from religious tradition, and articulated in reference to moral values, are intelligible and often compelling to villagers of all ages and educational levels.

What then are these developmental aims and how are they expressed? We examine them here in the context of the Dharma, because it is the Buddhist tradition to which most Sarvodayans belong and from which the Movement's leaders took inspiration; but these goals can be conveyed in terms of other faiths too, as Sarvodaya demonstrates in the Hindu, Christian, and Muslim communities where it works.

AWAKENING

It is the chief premise of the Movement that the notion of development can only be meaningful in terms of human fulfillment. While this fulfillment involves the production and consumption of goods, it entails a great deal more—such as the unfolding of the potential for

wisdom and compassion. While present conditions neither reflect nor
encourage this potential, it is real and can be awakened. In the Dharma
this awakening to one's true nature is the ultimate goal of existence,
exemplified for all in the enlightenment of the Lord Buddha under the
Bo tree. That is why Ariyaratna, the Movement's founder took the
term Sarvodaya, by which Gandhi had meant the uplift or welfare of
all, and, returning to its Sanskrit roots, reinterpreted it as the
"awakening of all."

Since *udaya* means awakening, and *sarva* means all, entire, or
total, the Movement's name is given a dual meaning. In addition to the
awakening of everybody, it denotes the awakening of the total human
personality. Indeed, the transformation of personality—the "building
of a new person"—is presented as the chief aim of the Movement.
Ariyaratna consistently stresses this, declaring that "the chief objective
of Sarvodaya is personality awakening"—that is, "with the effort of
the individual as well as with help from others, to improve oneself to
the highest level of well-being."[1]

> This definition of development goes beyond those that confine them-
> selves to measuring gross national products, growth rates, per-capita
> income, and even the latest measure called the Physical Quality of
> Life Index.... It represents the process [necessary for] total
> happiness.[2]

AWAKING TO INTERDEPENDENCE

Implicit in this goal is the belief that a root problem of poverty is a
sense of powerlessness. While most modern planners would view the
goal of spiritual awakening as idealistic and irrelevant, the Sarvodaya
Movement sees any development program as unrealistic which does
not recognize and alleviate the psychological impotence gripping the
rural poor. Sarvodaya believes that by tapping their innermost beliefs
and values, one can awaken people to their *swashakti* (personal power)
and *janashakti* (collective or people's power).

It sees this awakening taking place, not in monastic solitude, but in
social, economic and political interaction. While many capitalists and
Marxists take spiritual goals to be quietistic, mystical, drawing one off
onto private quests, Sarvodaya's goal and process of awakening pulls
one headlong into the "real" world and into the Movement's multi-
faceted programs for health, food, education, and productive enterprise. These programs are undertaken because people's basic material
needs must be met if they are to develop their potential; as was said by
the Buddha, who devoted a good portion of his teachings to economic
concerns, one cannot listen to the Dharma on an empty stomach.

Furthermore, in working together to meet these needs, people gain

---

[1]A.T. Ariyaratna in *Dana*, September 1980, p. 2.
[2]_____, *In Search of Development*, p. 32.

wisdom about the interdependence of life. This is important to Buddhists, because the interconnectedness and relativity of all phenomena—which is called "dependent co-arising" (paticca samuppada)—is the most central and distinctive doctrine of their religion. Its centrality, even in development work, is reflected in Ariyaratna's words: "A Sarvodaya worker learns to understand intellectually and to experience spiritually the interrelationship that exists between different manifestations of the living world."[3]

Because reality is seen as dependently co-arising, or systemic in nature, each and every act is understood to have an effect on the larger web of life, and the process of development is perceived as being multidimensional. One's personal awakening (purushodaya) is integral to the awakening of one's village (gramodaya), and both play integral roles in deshodaya and vishvodaya, the awakening of one's country and one's world. Being interdependent, these developments do not occur sequentially, in a linear fashion, but synchronously, each abetting and reinforcing the other through multiplicities of contacts and currents, each subtly altering the context in which other events occur.

A chief point to be stressed again here is that Sarvodaya's engagement of the people's religious traditions and aspirations is not instrumental to its work of community development, nor is it a means to attract them to the Movement, but rather the reverse. Community development is seen as the means for helping the people realize goals that are essentially religious.

That this represents the tacit assumption of most trained district and village-level organizers is evident when one watches and listens to them at work. Villagers are continually challenged to become more than they were—in their self-image and in their relations with others. To quote a few of these organizers:

> Your village may boast of having a post office, telephones, electricity...but that is not what constitutes being developed. Development is in your head, your mind.

> Here [in a shramadana camp] you find out what you can become. Leave behind your old conflicts, fears, and laziness, and discover your real strength and unity.

> It's not enough to parrot Sarvodaya philosophy, we've got to live it. Our revolution has got to be spiritual; no amount of tricking will get us there.

This belief in the "spiritual" nature of the "revolution" is what appears to distinguish Sarvodaya in the eyes of many of its young organizers, especially those who were active in the 1971 Insurgency. That traumatic event, initiated by the youth wing of the pro-Peking

---

[3] Ibid. p. 33.

THE FOUR NOBLE TRUTHS
OF VILLAGE AWAKENING*

The Dependent Co-Arising of a Decadent and a Sarvodaya Village

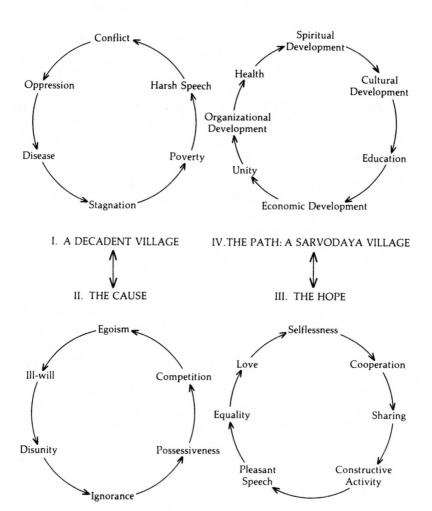

I. A DECADENT VILLAGE   IV. THE PATH: A SARVODAYA VILLAGE

II. THE CAUSE   III. THE HOPE

*Adapted from Sarvodaya charts.
Note: Some illustrations in Sarvodaya literature transpose a few of the factors between I and II; they are arranged here to distinguish symptoms I from deeper causes II, in keeping with the gist of Sarvodaya and Buddhist teachings. (Note also how the wheels of co-arising change direction when the Movement enters the scene.)

SARVODAYAN DEFINITION OF DEVELOPMENT
Goals and Sources

(Dhanagara = Land of Plenty)

(Dharmadveepa = Isle of Righteousness)

EACH ASPECT OF DEVELOPMENT SUPPORTS ALL THE OTHERS

SOCIAL

GOALS OF DEVELOPMENT	SOURCES IN THE DHARMA
Equality	Teachings of tolerance, compassion, and dependent co-arising. Example of Buddha as teacher, healer and reformer
Solidarity	
Education°	
Health°	

ECONOMIC

GOALS OF DEVELOPMENT	SOURCES IN THE DHARMA
Production of goods°*	Right livelihood, right effort, generosity, self restraint.
Conservation of resources	
Cooperative methods	
Appropriate consumption	

POLITICAL

GOALS OF DEVELOPMENT	SOURCES IN THE DHARMA
Decentralized	Rules and practices of early Sangha; teachings on nonviolence, tolerance, and karma.
Participation in decision-making	
Nonviolence	
Freedom from coercion	

MORAL

GOALS OF DEVELOPMENT	SOURCES IN THE DHARMA
No killing	The Five Precepts
No stealing	
No lying	
No sexual misconduct	
No drug abuse	

CULTURAL

GOALS OF DEVELOPMENT	SOURCES IN THE DHARMA
Harmony in relationships	Four Principles of group conduct; Four Abodes, indigenous art forms
Artistic expression in song, dance, poetry, architecture...	

SPIRITUAL

GOALS OF DEVELOPMENT	SOURCES IN THE DHARMA
Awakening from greed, hatred, and delusion into pure awareness of truth and compassion	Four Noble Truths, dependent co-arising, meditation

°Modern development goals usually limited to these.
*Modern economic goals usually limited to these.

Communist Party, drew on the desperation and idealism of a generation of university and high-school students. An indeterminate but
substantial number of these former insurgents, including young people
who were tried and jailed for their participation in the violence, are
now full-time Sarvodaya workers. Their comments to me indicate that
they assess the value of the Movement in the light of their past
experience, and that the value they see is both ideological and
practical:

> I tell my communist friends, I know how you work, because I was
> one of you. It is all talk, talk, talk. In Sarvodaya we *act . . . now . . .* we
> make shramadanas, training programs, preschools. We don't divide
> people, we show them how they can change.
>
> (*District coordinator, former insurgent*)

That notion that real social change requires personal change, a
notion conveyed in songs, slogans, murals, training courses, and
organizing methods, is anchored in Sarvodaya's creative interpretation
of traditional religious doctrine. In this respect Sarvodaya's ideology
can be seen as a "social gospel" form of Buddhism, stressing the
socioeconomic aspects and implications of the Buddha's teachings, and
presenting them as a challenge for villagers to take responsibility for
change.

The Four Noble Truths

The Movement's use of Buddhist teachings stands in contrast to
the Buddhist Marxism articulated by some Sinhalese monks in the
1950s and 1960s, who tended to present the Dharma as a form of dia-
lectical materialism. Sarvodaya's call to social engagement keeps the
spiritual factor preeminent—both in adducing the roots of inequity
and in defining the goals of development.

Its distinctive approach can be seen in the way it features and
interprets the Buddha's Four Noble Truths. The dictum of the First
Noble Truth, that "there is suffering," is translated concretely into
"there is a decadent village" and used as a means of consciousness-
raising. It serves to help the villagers focus on the actual conditions
prevailing in their community, on its poverty, conflict, and disease.
The importance of confronting these facts of life is reflected in Sarvodaya's style of organizing. Instead of coming in to present a predetermined project or "solution" to local problems, organizers first
instigate a village gathering where the village people, out of their own
experience, consider together their own situation and needs. Meeting
with the object of selecting a common work project, the "family
gathering" serves as a lens through which all those present can see more
clearly—and through each other's eyes as well—the present conditions

of the village, including the scope of its needs and internal conflicts.

At first glance it might seem reductionistic, especially to religionists, to present in such social terms the *dukkha* or suffering that the Buddha said we must recognize and confront. But in Sarvodaya's philosophy and approach the psycho-spiritual roots of this social suffering are made crystal-clear. The Second Noble Truth, which in Scripture declares that craving (*tanha*) is the cause of suffering, is presented by the Movement in terms of the egocentricity, greed, distrust, and competition that erode village energies. Each of these factors comes down to the individual's sense of separateness and selfishness. In the training of village organizers, these human failings are noted as having been exacerbated by the practices and attitudes of former colonial powers, and especially by the acquisitiveness bred by capitalism.

The Third Noble Truth, as traditionally formulated, affirms that craving, and therefore suffering, can cease—it is the hope at the heart of Buddhism. Sarvodaya presents this hope concretely in affirming that the village can reawaken and find its potential as a vigorous, unified, and caring community. No inexorable fate condemns people to live in apathy, sloth, distrust, or greed; for their actions, like their thoughts and words, are ultimately of their own choice. Action, choice—those, Ariyaratna reminds his Movement, are the original meaning of karma: just as our lives are conditioned by past deeds, so can they be remade by our present acts. All hinges on our will, on the choice that is present to us moment by moment.

The Eightfold path, which constitutes the Fourth Noble Truth, offers the principles by which to make such choices. Right Understanding and Right Intention arise as we understand the systemic nature of life, the interdependence between self and other, mind and body; and Right Speech arises as we give expression to this with honesty and compassion. Right Action, Right Livelihood, and Right Effort are no longer abstract notions, but become as immediate and tangible as today's collaboration in cleaning the village well or digging latrines, and Right Mindfulness is given a similarly social thrust. As a Sarvodaya trainer expresses it:

> Right Mindfulness—that means stay open and alert to the needs of the village. . . . Look to see what is needed—latrines, water, road. . . Try to enter the minds of the people, to listen behind their words. Practice mindfulness in the shramadana camp: is the food enough? are people getting wet? are the tools in order? is anyone being exploited?

The last aspect of the Eightfold Path, Right Concentration or *Samadhi*, is made present to the Movement through the moments of meditation that precede every meeting as well as through the optional meditation courses offered to its full-time workers.

The Four Noble Truths as reformulated are not taught to the people as a catechism; rather they are presented in symbols and graphics, on murals and posters, as reminders of what they experience already as they engage in the Movement's activities.

> Let them see first, listen second. Our philosophy is better understood in a shramadana than in a speech. Afterwards we give words to what they have experienced.
>
> *(District coordinator)*

Dana and the Sublime Abodes

How do you know if you are waking up? How, for that matter, do you go about that process? You practice *dana*, you enter the abodes.

Even more central to lay Buddhists than the Four Noble Truths is the concept and practice of *dana*, a venerable term which means both generosity and the act of giving, as well as the gift itself. Considered the most meritorious of all virtues, *dana* had, over the centuries, come to be identified with almsgiving to the Sangha or Order of Monks. Sarvodaya reclaimed its original scope by interpreting it to include the sharing of one's time, skills, goods, and energy with one's community. Villagers are not given sermons so much as opportunities to experience their own innate generosity. Whether it is a small child bringing her matchbox of rice to the Sarvodaya preschool or a landowner invited to give right of way for an access road through his tea estate, the operative assumption is that the act of giving empowers the giver and is the soil out of which mutual trust and respect can grow.

> Of course, her family is poor and of course we do not really need her little bit of rice or her betel leaf. But in giving it, she gets a new idea about herself.
>
> *(Shramadana organizer)*

Most frequently on the lips of Sarvodaya organizers and participants, and evoked at village gatherings, are the Sublime Abodes of the Buddha, also known as the *Brahmaviharas*. Embracing both the means and the measure of personal awakening, these are *Metta* (lovingkindness), *Karuna* (compassion), *Muditha* (joy in the joy of others), and *Upekkha* (equanimity). Like the Four Noble Truths, each of these is portrayed in terms of social interaction.

Sometimes explained in English as meaning "respect for all beings," *metta* or lovingkindness is presented by the Movement as the fundamental attitude that must be cultivated to develop motivation for service, capacity to work harmoniously with others, and, above all, the nonviolence that is a central premise of Sarvodaya. The Movement promotes it through sermon, song, and slogan, and also through the practice of the *metta* meditation, which is expected of all participants and accorded silence at the outset of every meeting, be it a community "family gathering" or a committee session on latrines. Summoning participants to develop the "boundless heart" of the Buddha, it can serve to ennoble menial tasks, defuse conflict, and inspire the giving of energy.

Metta is taken, furthermore, as an instrument for affecting the thoughts of others, and is used in such fashion by some of the clergy. A young Sarvodaya-trained monk went to settle in a village that had been a Communist stronghold and that initially opposed his work through abuse, open threats, and depredations on the newly reopened temple. His explanation to me of how he finally won the villagers' support did not feature any particular organizing strategy. Rather, he said,

> It was doing the *metta* meditation. . .every day before I went out and every night when I came back, sending the power of lovingkindness to my opponents. After two years most of the village was with me.

Compassion (*karuna*), the second Sublime Abode, is seen by the Movement as the translation of *metta* into action on behalf of others. It includes the concepts of service and "self-offering" that have been central to Sarvodaya since its inception.

> Feeling sorry for people is not enough. Act to help them.
> (*Shramadana guideline*)

> Nonviolence is more than not walking on insects in the road. It is to be of service to our fellow-beings.
> (*Sarvodaya organizer*)

Muditha, as defined by the Movement, is the joy one reaps in beholding the effects of this service. Whether these results are seen in a completed road to the village or in the altered lives of its inhabitants, they constitute the most tangible external reward gained by most Sarvodayans. But the Movement urges its workers not to be dependent on even these rewards, for their work may fail and is bound, in any case, to displease some parties and arouse opposition. Hence the importance of *upekkha*, equanimity in the face of praise or blame. It is a notion which helps preserve Sarvodaya workers from "burn-out."

> Don't be discouraged if they [villagers] seem not to care. We will teach them by *our* caring.
> (*Young trainer*)

> *Upekkha* is dynamite. It is surprising the energy that is released when you stop being so attached. . . . You discover how much can be accomplished when nothing is expected in return.
> (*District coordinator*)

A plethora of Buddhist stories, many drawn from the Jataka tales about earlier human and animal incarnations of the Buddha, illustrate these virtues in action. They are familiar to Sri Lankan Buddhists, and Sarvodaya monks often recount them again in preschools, youth groups, festive ceremonies, and the "family gatherings" that punctuate the work camps. They add substance and flavor to the notion of personal awakening.

If the Four Abodes are taken as signs and means of personal awakening, the Dharma also specifies four principles of social behavior (*Satara Sangraha Vastu*), which Sarvodaya upholds as pathways to community awakening. In addition to *dana*, whereby people come alive again to their capacity to give and receive from each other, these principles include *priyavachana*, literally translated as pleasant speech. Sarvodaya takes it to stress the subtle, far-reaching importance of the everyday language we use, in helping to avoid divisiveness and violence and in promoting mutual respect and a sense of equality. The third principle, *samanatmatha*, is social equality itself. Ariyaratna, who initiated his Movement in an outcaste village, reminds his fellow-Buddhists that discrimination on the basis of caste or class is a moral outrage that was rejected by the Lord Buddha himself. Over the centuries, under the influence of the Hindu subcontinent, caste practices insinuated into South Asian Buddhism, but they are rejected by Sarvodaya, where social equality remains fundamental to development work. The fourth and last of these ancient principles of social conduct is *arthachariya* or constructive work. Symbolized in the shramadana work camps, the sharing of labor is viewed as essential if persons and communities are to awaken to their potential and capacity for self-reliance.

SELF RELIANCE

As global economic patterns, with the centralizing effect of their markets, technologies, and capital investments, render rural populations poorer and more dependent, and as many large-scale assistance programs seem to have exacerbated this debilitating dependence on external factors, planners and theorists increasingly recognize the importance of local self-reliance as a development goal. Clearly, as we have seen from its genesis and history as a self-help movement, Sarvodaya has adopted this goal as central to its existence. What resources does it draw from religion to help it pursue this goal? What traditional values serve to legitimate and motivate villagers' efforts toward self-reliance?

In Sarvodaya, self-reliance is set within the larger goal of awakening and seen as integral to human fulfillment. Indeed, Ariyaratna presents them as virtually synonymous:

> The ideas of self-development, self-fulfillment, and self-reliance, all are understood in the single word *udaya* (awakening)....This is consistent with the Buddhist principle that salvation lies primarily in one's hands, be it an individual or a group.[4]

In appealing to Buddhist principles as fundamental to self-reliance, Ariyaratna is on firm ground. Of the world's great religious teachers, the Buddha was probably the least authoritarian and the most emphatic in urging his followers to rely on their own experience and on their own efforts. Both on the economic level, through his teachings of Right Effort and Right Livelihood, and on the spiritual level through his admonitions to "Come see for yourselves" and "Be ye lamps unto yourselves," he urged people to take responsibility for their lives. These admonitions are echoed now in the words of some Sarvodaya trainers—and this despite the traditionally hierarchical cast of Sinhalese culture. To quote one of them, as he expounded Sarvodaya concepts to a group of new trainees, "Don't take *my* word for it. Think it out for yourselves. You will see how it works."

The Dharma also offers historical models of local self-reliance in decision-making, for in its early centuries the Sangha (Order) was highly decentralized into local autonomous communities, and the vast wave of Buddhism spread across Asia with no central locus of authority, with no Rome or Jerusalem ever evolving as center of control. This model of self-governance is now being adopted by Sarvodaya as it pursues a policy of radical decentralization. The national headquarters at Moratuwa has divested itself of control over budget and program, according it first to the regional coordinating centers and now progressively to the incorporated Village Awakening Councils. The opening lines of its 1981 Annual Service Report convey both its attitude and the risks it is ready to undertake:

> The policy of the last few years...distributes the power exercised at the centre until the centre exercises no administrative and no financial control of the units at the periphery.... The faith placed in a set of very young men and women with relatively little academic training but with plenty of self-confidence born of living and working with the villagers to usher in a Sarvodaya social order has been amply justified. A few of them have not been able to keep up the pace. But this was not entirely unexpected.

To help villagers move out of patterns of apathy and dependence, Movement organizers challenge the villagers, from the moment of the first meeting, to participate in decision-making and to take some

---

[4] _____, *Collected Works I*, p. 26.

action—no matter how small or menial—in meeting a local need. When the action is finite enough for its success to be predictable and measurable, it can begin to build a sense of power—both personal power (*swashakti*) and people's power (*janashakti*).

> You say you have waited two years for the government to clean that canal. You can keep on waiting, while your fields bake. But where is your own power? You won't find it sitting around till the government does it for you. Your power is not in Colombo; it is in you, in your heads and hands.
>
> (*Shramadana organizer*)

Given its emphasis on local self-reliance, it is not surprising that Sarvodaya has been a pioneer of appropriate village-level technology in Sri Lanka, constructing and experimenting with windmills, biogas generators, gravity-fed water systems. The Movement appeals to the Buddhist virtues of thrift and self-restraint in consumption, as it urges its workers to use cheap local resources. Out of an abundantly available weed it has developed the nutritious conjee-leaf soup for its community kitchens, out of banana-tree juice a tough mortar for mud-walled housing, out of palm products ingredients for roofing sheets and laundry soap. The Buddha's teaching of Right Livelihood is, of course, relevant to the Movement's efforts to develop the village industries and community shops that make and sell such products, and to keep their overhead low so that they can survive in today's market.

Self-reliance is also a goal in Sarvodaya's work with children. Pre-school programs (under way in over two thousand villages) have long been a dominant feature of the Movement; this is partly because they are non-controversial and easy to mount, and because they serve as an opening wedge for community organizing. But they are also undertaken because they build the "psychological infrastructure" which Ariyaratna and his colleagues see as essential to long-term development. This last objective is conspicuous in their innovative, non-authoritarian methods. Contrasting with educational styles found elsewhere in the country, these methods foster the child's self-reliance in three ways: 1) through creative, energetic play using messy materials and large motor-muscles, 2) through the repeated offering of choice, and 3) through opportunities to perform and help at village work camps. Even Sarvodaya workers who are uninvolved with children's services recognize the importance of this approach; to quote two, both male:

> Just as we work from the village up to make Sri Lanka strong again, so we must work from the infant up. All the world's great men were little once, got their start in infancy. The little child can understand a

lot, he's got a good head. Give him the experiences he needs to develop his mind.

(Shramadana trainer)

Don't do for the child what he can do for himself. Don't over-help. That way he can find his *swashakti* [own power].

(Shramadana organizer)

Given the fact that Sarvodaya's finances have been heavily dependent on foreign assistance, and that the self-help and appropriate technology programs I describe have been supported by Dutch, German, and American agencies, the question has been raised as to how seriously the Movement takes this matter of self-reliance. In reply to this question, Ariyaratna makes several points. In the light of the structural inequalities at work in our world today, and considering the state of material and psychological dependence existing in the impoverished countries, self-reliance, he says, is a relative term, and not to be equated with financial independence. Until a just economic order prevails, such independence is a chimera, and "for the haves to turn towards the have-nots and tell them to be self-reliant is a very superficial statement."[5]

To generate the process of awakening, resources are needed which, unlike other projects, cannot be measured in cost-benefit terms. Furthermore, the Movement's budget, where foreign aid features so largely (about eighty percent), does not include the time, labor, skills, and gifts in kind that Sarvodaya workers and villagers provide at no cost. When these are computed, however, a different picture emerges. A current Dutch-sponsored study reveals that shramadana camps, for example, create capital many times in excess of the financial input. Thus in one year Sarvodayans built three times as much roadway as the government did, and at one-eighteenth of the cost.[6] Such computations do not include the "human capital" these efforts create—in terms of motivation, mutual trust, self-esteem, and leadership skills. But Sarvodaya considers the human capital equally valuable, for it is intrinsic to a people's capacity for genuine self-reliance in the long term.

NATIONAL SELF-ESTEEM

It is hard for a community or a people to release its energies—and experience its self-reliance—if it is pervaded by a sense of unworthiness and cultural inferiority. Sarvodaya's summons to "wake up" goes hand in hand with a reaffirmation of the strength and beauty of Sri Lanka's indigenous culture. Its appeals to national self-esteem draw from the

[5] _____, "What is Self-Reliance?", *Annual Service Report 1980-1981* (Sarvodaya Shramadana Movement, April 1981), p. 70.
[6] Sarvodaya Research Institute, *Integrated Rural Development* (Ratmalana: 1982), Chapter 3.

religious heritage that bred the grandeur of this culture.

In traditional, postcolonial societies, the affirmation of culture and the affirmation of religion are commensurate. The revival of Sinhalese Buddhism that took place in the late nineteenth century had a nationalistic flavor; challenging the people to cast off their emulation of the colonizers' ways, it drew on the need for cultural pride and renewed it at the same time. In similar fashion, Sarvodaya's community-development form of Buddhism presents itself as a reclamation of the nation's heritage. The glories of the past, when Ceylon was *Dharmadveepa* (island of righteousness) and *Dhanagara* (treasury of wealth or "granary of the East," as it was known abroad), are evoked in speeches and songs which summon the population to the noble task of building anew on its ancient strengths.

> People laughed to see me working like a coolie, especially when the sacks of milk powder I was carrying leaked down my back. But I remembered I was working for *Dharmadveepa* and *Dhanagara*, and the ridicule did not bother me.
> *(Young trainer to new recruits)*

These images are explicitly used to counter the feelings of cultural inferiority that often result from contact with "developed" countries, through tourism and imported goods and advertising. The great Ceylonese reformer, Dharmapala, who at the turn of the century called on his countrypeople to reject slavish imitation of Western dress and manners, is an oft-quoted inspiration to Sarvodayans. They see their prestigious leaders appear in banian and sarong; they hear their trainers remind them:

> How silly it is to ape ways that are not suitable . . . . as foolish as using forks instead of fingers, or wearing the tight trousers. Sarongs are more comfortable and efficient. They are cooler in the heat, easier for movement and for answering the calls of nature.

This cultural affirmation is not only national but *rural*, for villagers' feelings of backwardness result also from contact with urban, Westernized Sri Lankans. Even among Sarvodaya staff-persons the lure of "modern" appearance and behavior is strong. Some are tempted to acquire status, in their own and the villagers' eyes, by imitating bureaucratic behavior—using staff vehicles, dressing Western, flaunting "official files." But these are usually criticized, and ridiculed:

> J. and E. used a Sarvodaya jeep to go to Kandy, when they could have gone by bus or train. They were just showing off. That is not the Sarvodaya spirit.

> K. came to the shramadana, but he wanted to stay clean and go

around carrying his papers and checking off lists of names. We said
he could leave, because there is no room in Sarvodaya for a "file
Mahattea" [file gentleman].

The Movement fosters a sense of cultural pride through repeated
allusions to past glory (in speeches and songs about Dharmadveepa
and Dhanagara), through efforts to clean and restore indigenous
monuments (from village temple compounds to the sacred precincts of
the ancient royal stupas), and through emphasis on traditional custom
(from village rituals, like the blessing of the fields, to the practicing of
"reverencing" one's parents). All of these have religious roots and
religious flavor.

In addition to these, another factor now fosters a sense of cultural
pride among Sarvodayans, especially the more sophisticated and
thoughtful of the organizers. That is the knowledge that their work in
the Movement has meaning for the rest of the world, in revealing the
true nature of development. For *vishvodaya* or world awakening—and
not just for itself—Sri Lanka can become again, they would believe, an
"island of righteousness."

ECONOMICS OF SUFFICIENCY

The awakening of personality, and the revitalization of rural
culture in which this awakening can take place, entail economic as well
as cultural goals. They involve economic pursuits and structures that
foster the feelings of self-worth and self-reliance and that serve to
integrate, rather than disperse, the energies of the local community.

The goals Sarvodaya sets for economic development are rooted,
and often explicitly so, in religious belief. The Buddha's original teachings on economic values and ethics are being brought out and dusted
off; from the *Vyaggha Pajja* to the *Kutadanta* sutras, they serve to
offer, and to validate, an alternative to classical Western economics.[7]
From the perspective of the Dharma, economic interest includes not
only production and profit, but also the "externalities" of human and
environmental costs. The conservation of material resources, their
humane use, and their equitable distribution are taken as legitimate
and indeed preeminent concerns.

If the Buddha taught that craving is at the root of human suffering,
then so too are patterns of production and consumption that inflame
this craving. Sarvodayans take this teaching as indicative of the
weakness and indeed the pathology of the capitalist system, with its
inherent reliance on the creation of felt needs and its promotion of
acquisitiveness. From the perspective of the Dharma, modest con-

[7] These are spelled out, *inter alia*, in Ariyaratna, *Collected Works* (Netherlands,
Sarvodaya Research Institute, 1979); Joanna Macy, "The Distinctiveness of
Buddhist Ethics" (*Journal of Religious Ethics*, Spring 1979); E.F. Schumacher,
Small is Beautiful (New York: Harper & Row, 1973); and E. Sarkisyanz, *Bud-
dhist Roots of the Burmese Revolution* (The Hague: Martinus Nijhoff, 1965).

sumption is not only conservative of resources, but essential to spiritual health and self-reliance. To clarify the purposes of a just social order, as well as to set parameters for appropriate consumption and economic enterprise, Ariyaratna and his colleagues formulated a list of Ten Basic Human Needs, which, as I noted in Chapter Two, go beyond material requirements for food, water, clothing, health care, housing, and energy, and include educational, social, cultural, and spiritual needs. Attention to the non-material needs sets the material ones in perspective, as the support but not the purpose of life.

These, together with the Buddha's teaching of Right Livelihood, set human labor within a context of character formation and life-enhancement that surpasses its worth in terms of income generation alone.

> When we look at our basic human needs, we see what livelihood really is. It is not just getting a job; it is working to meet these needs.
> *(District-level organizer)*

Because Sarvodaya refuses to divorce the economic from the spiritual goals of humankind, it is as critical of the socialist as of the capitalist model of development. With their common focus on growth in production and their top-heavy, top-down structures, both systems leave "a very insignificant place for the individual," as N. Ratnapala, director of the Sarvodaya Research Institute writes:

> The contradictions [of both socialist and capitalist models] emanate from their inability to understand the twin or dual character of development, i.e. it involves both the individual and the group, and it must satisfy both economic and spiritual needs.[8]

Even in a proposal devoted to promoting a village industries scheme, Sarvodaya's staff states that "rural industrialization is not our first objective." That first objective, they say, is the "total well-being" of the people, moral and cultural as well as economic. From the perspective of Sarvodaya, those dimensions of well-being are often inseparable, because they conduce to village integration and increased vitality. In a "model village" settlement in a former coconut plantation, a Sarvodaya worker organized a shramadana to build some houses. As a government agricultural officer reports:

> The people in this village used to be very lazy. They didn't take care of the trees and only had energy for stealing. Then in the shramadana the men worked together learning to make bricks. Now they are making and selling bricks to other villages...and putting the profit into fertilizer for joint cultivation of the coconuts.

Programs creating jobs that draw villagers to remote work places, like free-trade or Investment Promotion Zones, are not, from this

---

[8]N. Ratnapala on p. 2 of his introduction to Ariyaratna, *In Search of Development*.

perspective, truly "economic"; for they erode the villagers' true security, which is inseparable from their family and community relations. It is this security, along with the self-respect and harmony generated by constructive work, that is seen by Sarvodaya as the essential value of economic endeavor. Or, to use the Burmese Buddhist term employed by E.F. Schumacher, it is this "sufficiency"— an economic base sufficient to the pursuit of enlightenment—that is the goal of economic activity.

The Buddhist principle of *arthacharya*, or constructive activity, includes, as we noted, both voluntary and remunerative work, giving equal dignity to unpaid efforts, and indeed exalting them as *dana* or gifts to the public weal. While Sarvodaya seeks to promote income-generating activities in the villages, recognizing their desperate and growing penury, it declines to judge the value of human energy in terms of cash earned. The free sharing of labor, skills, and time is seen as ennobling and necessary for both the individual and society. By virtue of that belief and its practice in shramadana, Sarvodaya erodes the division between the formal and nonformal sectors of the economy, which in our time tends to rob non-remunerated work of its dignity.

> We had traditions based on trust, like *rajakariya*, where we gave to the common good. Now people only want to work for wage and profit. And look! That does not enrich us, and it does not satisfy us either.
>
> (*Sarvodaya trainer*)

Such a vision of development—with its rejection of a capital-intensive, high-technology, and import-based economy—is clearly at odds not only with classical Western notions, but also with the policies pursued by the present Sri Lankan government. It is noteworthy that Sarvodaya's use of religion in conveying this vision permits it to do so in a way that appears less oppositional, and perhaps less threatening. It is hard to take issue with invocations of Buddhist teachings and scriptures, especially when the party in power also cloaks itself in an aura of Buddhist piety.

POLITICAL NONPARTISANSHIP AND SOCIAL UNITY

A chief cause of village stagnation, in the eyes of the Movement, consists of the conflicts that fragment human energies and discourage joint action, conflicts bred by caste, class, and especially party politics. Feuding and backbiting, fomented by petty politicization at the local level, often mire even the best public programs, and can stalemate local organizations from the Rural Development Society to the Lanka

Mahila Samiti (National Women's Society).

Talking with villagers in over thirty localities, I asked how Sarvo-daya differs from other organizations. Almost unanimously their replies singled out, as the Movement's most distinguishing feature, its nonpartisan character. By the same token the chief result of its activi-ties was seen to be an increased sense of community within the village. The nonpartisan nature of the Movement is clearly basic to its effective-ness in engaging the trust of the people. This is particularly significant in a country and under a regime where local social and economic efforts are as heavily politicized as they are in Sri Lanka today.

> We turned to Sarvodaya and asked the District center to help us organize our rebuilding, because everyone else, including the Gram Sevaka, [government extension agent at village level], had his own party interests and his own party favorites. The fighting kept us at a standstill. When Sarvodaya came in, we could work together.
>
> *(Member of model village)*

The high priority Sarvodaya puts on unity stems from its vision of the "awakening of all". Inspiration is drawn from the Buddha, who in his own time assailed social divisions bred by caste or class, by narrow allegiances or doctrinaire opinions. His egalitarian inclusivity and tolerance are reemphasized today as essential to successful community action.

Sarvodaya's record success in maintaining such a nonpartisan stance in today's Sri Lanka is due to the explicitness of its philosophy on this point and to two other factors as well. One is the skill of its leadership and local organizers in keeping aloof from party politics:

> Never invite a politician to your first shramadana. Wait till the villagers have a sense of their own power, otherwise he's likely to make them feel dependent on *him*.

> No, I never tell villagers how I voted.
>
> *(District coordinators)*

The other factor in maintaining the nonpartisan character of the Move-ment is its involvement on the grassroots level of the least partisan institutions. The Sarvodaya Movement's activities are most frequently introduced into a village by the clergy and its meetings most often held on the premises of the local religious establishment.

This use of ecclesiastical personnel and sites might be expected to cause some divisiveness, from a religious if not a political standpoint; but, in my own observations, I did not find this to be the case. Pictures of the Buddha, Jesus, Krishna, and the Muslim moon and minaret hang side by side in some Sarvodaya rural centers; and where different faiths are present in a given locality their prayers intermingle in the "family gatherings," as do their clergy in the work projects. Even on Christian premises, which are seen in Sri Lanka as the most exclusivist, this has occurred—as when, for example, a Roman Catholic priest agreed to have a Buddha statue installed in his church school for the duration of a Sarvodaya shramadana, and to have the meetings co-officiated by Buddhist monks. I know of no instances where such ecumenicity caused confusion or conflict among participants; indeed the reverse seems to be true, with villagers, especially young people, responding favorably to the opportunity to share traditions of other faiths.

Privately and separately I asked the three Christian women in the training program I attended what their responses were to the predominantly Buddhist flavor of the organization. Did they feel in any way excluded, overshadowed? To my surprise, each volunteered reasons why she did not mind being in the minority:

> Well, there are Christian prayers, too, in the Paule Hamua (family gathering). As you have seen, they are recited first.

> It has been good to learn something of Buddhist teachings, especially about community awakening. I thought the monks just sat in their temples receiving dana, and did not care about changing things.

> I like the meditation best [of all the training]; I never did it before and I think it is important for feeling strong.

In a socially fragmented, urban slum area not far from my village home, the first Sarvodaya shramadana was organized by monks to clean and repair a historic Buddhist temple. Because they had gone house-to-house to invite all local families to participate in it as a community project, some Muslims came too. They entered the shrine for the first time, and quietly gave a Sarvodaya monk small gifts of cash toward the work camp's collective meal.

A sense of unity between the Sinhalese and Tamil populations remains a Sarvodaya goal that has been more difficult to pursue. That is because not only religious differences, but social, linguistic, historic, and political conflicts separate the Buddhist Sinhalese from the Hindu Tamils, and have engendered bitter and sometimes violent communal strife. Sarvodaya has been criticized by both sides, for being either too identified with Buddhism or too active among Hindus. Separatist Tamils view with little enthusiasm the Movement's integrated programs and its caste-free policies (caste practices being far more entrenched in Hindu society), and accuse it of serving the cause of Buddhist hegemony. Meanwhile fringe nationalist elements on the other side have accused it of compromising Sinhalese Buddhist solidarity.

Within the organization itself, however, these communal tensions are transcended. Sinhalese and Tamil district-level organizers meet frequently to coordinate Sarvodaya's national and regional programs. This collaboration breeds a familiarity and mutual trust that motivate and enable them to play a mediating role between the two populations, defusing their fears and frictions, as I saw the district coordinators do in Jaffna and Anuradhapura. After the 1981 "emergency," when communal conflict provoked the imposition of martial law, the government requested Ariyaratna to step in. Undertaking a non-stop tour of the more sensitive areas, the Sarvodaya founder initiated the Harmony Project, in which teams of young people are exchanged between Sinhalese and Tamil villages—as village-level workers and goodwill ambassadors. Now, even more than before, Sarvodaya is the one organization that most effectively bridges the country's two chief populations.

IV

Religion and Community Organizing Methods

IN THE SARVODAYA MOVEMENT, AS WE HAVE SEEN, RELIGION plays a key role in defining the nature and purpose of development, doing so in terms that are meaningful to local people. Religion also serves effectively as a resource in shaping the Movement's more effective organizing techniques. That is the method by which it contacts the villagers, transmits its aims, and engages them in its programs. Most of these methods originated in shramadana, the voluntary village work projects which initiated the Movement in 1958 and which continue to function as its central organizing strategy. These have spawned behaviors and techniques that carry over into other types of Sarvodaya work as well. That being the case, and for the sake of clarity and brevity, these techniques will be examined here in the context of a shramadana camp.

SHRAMADANA CAMPS

What are the resources of the have-nots? The capacity to think, to feel, to work. This *shrama* can either be exchanged for payment or be intelligently shared for common benefit. In the existing production relationships for mere survival one has to sell one's *shrama*, but to create new non-exploitative relationships one has to learn the art and science of sharing it—of shramadana. Self-reliance cannot exist without sharing.

(*A.T. Ariyaratna*)[1]

While shramadana can refer to any voluntary activity, the term is used more specifically to denote the work camps the Movement sponsors as an organizing device within a given locality. It has sponsored some 13,700 camps in the last ten years.[2]

[1]A. T. Ariyaratna, "What is Self-Reliance?," *Dana* (September 1980), p. 3.
[2]Sarvodaya Research Institute, *Integrated Rural Development*, Chap. 3.

In the early years the Movement was known simply as the Shramadana Movement. While its camps were initially inspired by reports of church-sponsored work camps in Europe, they have, from the outset, differed from that model in important ways. The kind of work camp that is familiar in the West, and that has also been undertaken by Gandhians in India, consists (1) mainly of young people, most of whom (2) come in from other localities to (3) labor on projects designed by the sponsoring organization. By contrast the Sarvodaya version is a local community effort from start to finish, engaging people of all ages, and from all sectors of the village, in the selection and organization of the project as well as in the provision of labor. Its purpose, furthermore—and this is a central point—goes far beyond the accomplishment of a material task, to the development of local initiative and leadership. It is also the primary means by which Sarvodaya recruits its cadres. Estimates by veteran organizers of the proportion of their fellow-workers brought into the Movement through shramadana—i.e., whose initial exposure to Sarvodaya occurred at a camp—range from 60% to 90%.

The number of such camps is hard to judge with any precision, since some of the districts, including very active ones, have not sent in their shramadana figures; but those that did so reported a total of 3,437 shramadana camps in the single year ending March 1981, with a participation of 178,220 people, one twelfth of whom were Sarvodaya workers.[3]

The genius of shramadana is its capacity to provide a model for the society that Sarvodaya would build. It offers participants the chance to experience—in action and in the present—the kinds of psychological, social, and physical interaction that the Movement considers integral to village awakening. It is an island in time where people can see themselves and each other in a new light. Even if, after it is all over, the village seems to revert to business-as-usual, it is never quite the same; for the experience of sharing and working together is not forgotten, nor are the skills acquired in organizing the event erased. Indeed, the experience and the skills often catalyze subsequent activities—collective ventures, such as cooperative marketing or preschools or literacy classes, on which villagers are then moved to embark.

We build the road and the road builds us.

(Sarvodaya slogan)

It is not only the Buddhist word *dana* that suggests a religious component to the activity. The majority of camps are organized out of or in conjunction with the local temple—or, in the case of non-

---

[3]*Ibid.*, and Sarvodaya Shramadana Movement, *Annual Service Report*, March 1981, p. 51.

Buddhist communities, the kovil, church, or mosque. Preliminary meetings in the weeks before the camp are usually held in the preaching hall, which also serves as focus for meals and "family gatherings" during the shramadana itself, and lodging for participants from other villages. The camp, furthermore, is punctuated with rituals— from the chants, meditation, and prayers at each thrice-daily "family gathering" to the procession with banners and monks to the work site. At virtually all shramadanas clergy are present, officiating at the meetings and advising the food and work teams; in addition to the monk or priest who helped organize the event, others often come from different temples.

All this—the use of religious premises, rituals, personnel—makes the shramadana a quasi-religious event, which in turn serves Sarvodaya's development goals in several ways:

1. It legitimizes the event in the eyes of traditional villagers, thereby sanctioning even among the more conservative elements the notion of grassroots community action. In many villages Sarvodaya organizers start with a camp devoted to repairing or cleaning the temple, it being easier to recruit volunteer labor for such meritorious activities; then, once the villagers have experienced the power and excitement of a shramadana, they are ready to consider more ambitious community projects.

2. It encourages participation, especially of women and girls whose families are more willing to let them join an effort when it is sponsored by the temple and attended by clergy.

3. It dramatizes Sarvodaya's philosophy of development with its emphasis on spiritual awakening, and provides an appropriate and authenticating setting for recounting the stories that convey the social teachings of the Buddha.

4. It taps the intellectual and educational resources of the clergy, as well as their prestige and time; and

5. It provides a nonpartisan context for community action, conducive to the unity Sarvodaya seeks to build in villages often torn with dissension and fragmented by politics.

This last point cannot be overemphasized. In researching the effects of shramadana, I asked villagers what, if any, changes they noted in their community after a work camp had been held. Almost without exception, and regardless of size, area, kind of project undertaken, or even extent of Sarvodaya follow-up, the replies singled out—as the greatest change engendered—a new sense of unity and cohesion in the village. This achievement is considered by most organizers as more important than the specific material task accomplished. It fosters the internal communication, and the mutual trust and initiative, that are required for any grassroots development effort.

> The road we build may wash away, but the attitudes we build do
> not.
>   (*District coordinator*)

> After the shramadana my family decided to stay instead of returning
> to Colombo. For the first time since we came to live here two years
> ago, we feel we have friends. It is a place we want to be in.
>   (*Mother in new village settlement*)

Specific approaches and methods, as we shall see, foster this experience of community. Their effectiveness can be seen in the contrast between Sarvodayan and non-Sarvodayan shramadanas, for the Movement's labor-sharing camps became so popular after 1958 that they have been imitated by other organizations and by the government itself. In these cases the practice is generally removed from the spiritual context Sarvodaya gives it and cast in secular, purely task-oriented terms.

From my year's observations, shramadanas conducted by Sarvodaya generally show better results—in terms of attendance, morale, material contributions, and actual work performed—than shramadanas held under other auspices. The contrast is particularly vivid when the Movement is working on the same project as a group organized by non-Sarvodayans, as was the case on the road to Hiniduma in the summer months of 1979. There a collection of volunteers sponsored and recruited by the government was engaged at one end of the projected road. With numbers and support equivalent to that of the Sarvodaya group at the other end of the road, it was accomplishing less than half as much per day—until a Sarvodaya District Coordinator was persuaded to come in and take charge. He did so, bringing in Sarvodaya philosophy and process, and immediately the rate of work improved dramatically. He did more than *talk* to the participants about awakening *metta* and *Dharmadveepa*; he instituted practices by which these ideas could be internalized and experienced.

It is for this component of tactical ideology or philosophy-in-action that other organizations, having adopted shramadana, now turn again to Sarvodaya for guidance. So we see secular agencies, like the National Youth Service or the Ministry of Education, seeking to emulate practices that are largely religious in inspiration. Let us consider these practices as they relate to the sharing of labor, the sharing of food, the sharing of ideas, and the use of sharing language.

SHARING LABOR

To work side by side, on an immediate, physical, and often arduous task, permits people to experience the common basics that underlie their usual differences—differences of education, caste, class, sex, age, vocation, politics. These are temporarily eclipsed in the heat, dust, sweat, and laughter of slinging weeds from an obstructed irrigation canal or levering a boulder from a projected roadway. The labor is beneath no one's dignity because it is *dana*, a merit-gaining gift. In a Sarvodaya shramadana this experience and the pride of physical accomplishment are open to all—women as well as men, educated elite and landless laborers, children and grandparents too (the very young and the old bring tea, carry messages, smooth sand, pile weeds, give advice).

This inclusivity of all levels and segments of a village contrasts with shramadanas organized by other agencies, such as those of Rural Development Societies, which are usually limited to able-bodied males. Being more task-oriented these camps can be more effective in terms of the material objective, although this is not always the case. The government-sponsored contingent on the Hiniduma road was all male until the Sarvodaya coordinator, who took charge to improve the work rate, reorganized it to include women as well. In any event the impact on the community as a whole is less when the process is less widely shared. The village committees (youth groups, mothers' groups, children's groups, *et al.*, which Sarvodaya aims to catalyze in the course of a shramadana) derive much of their inspiration and momentum from this experience of giving labor.

The sharing of physical labor narrows the gap between villagers and bureaucrats. Sarvodaya leaders on the national and district level tell me they like to make time to attend a shramadana because it grounds and refreshes their energies.

> Going to shramadana—getting out there in the dirt—it connects me again with the real purpose of my work. All this paper, all these schedules, reports, meetings. . .I see the reason for it each time I do shramadana in a village. The people help me remember why I am doing what I do.
>
> *(District coordinator)*

Government extension agents are usually invited to shramadanas which Sarvodaya organizes in their areas. Rural Development officers, Gram Sevakas, Assistant Government Agents, officials from Ministries of Health or Education—they come to give speeches at the "family gatherings." But it is hard to remain an onlooker at a shramadana, and they often find themselves, with trousers and sleeves rolled up, joining the villagers as they cut the road or pile foundation rocks for the preschool. It is a learning experience for both parties, breeding trust on one side, respect on the other. As a mud-splattered Gram Sevaka said after a morning knee-deep in a canal, "I thought you were the most backward village in my area. Now I know better. You can teach the rest of them how to work together."

The investment of one's own labor brings a sense of ownership, a personal stake in the project. The Gram Sevaka quoted above returned to the village more frequently after the camp, experiencing a different connection with the people and their needs and hopes. The villagers who cut a road keep the culverts open when the rainstorms come; those who dug latrines in shramadana see that they are *used*—and with the government-supplied concrete slabs properly installed. A principal showed me the school roof that students had repaired, voluntarily and without being asked, after they had participated in a shramadana to clear the playground. Many government tree-planting schemes suffer from depredation and neglect, but that fate does not befall the seed-lings planted in a shramadana camp. Even the little children—who in the festival atmosphere helped prepare the holes and then carried over the government-supplied coconut seedlings, their stems reaching high over their heads—now faithfully bring water and shoo off the marauding goats and cows.

SHARING FOOD

The sharing of food is an intrinsic part of shramadana, for noon meals—and morning and evening meals, too, when the camp lasts longer than a day—are communal events. In a classic Sarvodaya shramadana they are not only consumed together, but collectively provided and prepared, with contributions solicited from all sectors of the village population regardless of caste or economic level. As many religious traditions attest, from Hindu *prasad* to the Christian sacrament of Eucharist, the celebratory partaking of common food generates a sense of community across all conventional social boun-daries. Here that sense is intensified through the collection of food from many households and its preparation in the temple compound or near the work site by teams of village women. Most veteran Sarvodaya organizers consider this sharing of food as important in building village unity as the joint gift of labor.

Sometimes money given to the Movement to assist in organizing shramadanas is used not only to pay for tools and transportation, but also to buy food for the event—either in bulk or in lunch packets from a local merchant. That is certainly easier than spending days going door-to-door collecting promises of food donations, and it is con-sidered necessary when the local population is very poor; but that expedient is viewed by some old-time organizers as counterproductive. It deprives the villagers of the added power and cohesion they can find in their own giving and in partaking of each other's food.

She is a day-laborer—and for rice for the shramadana she gave me more than she earns in a whole day. But it was worth it to her—and to us—for she feels important to the village now in a way she did not before.

(District coordinator)

With the progressive impoverishment of the rural population through job-loss and inflation, it is sometimes simply impossible, some organizers point out, to stage a shramadana meal on local contributions alone, and some bulk food items must be provided. Furthermore, the promise of a subsidized meal adds to the lure of the event. Yet experience shows the value of relying as much as possible on local contributions. In organizing one village's first shramadana, young Sarvodayans expected that the households they solicited would be reimbursed from funds they would receive from the Rural Development Ministry, since the work was on an irrigation canal, which the Ministry's Food For Work budget covered. Afterwards they learned that the money would not be forthcoming—but by then it seemed to make little difference. "But how can you pay for the food now?" I asked, when I returned to the scene. "Oh, it doesn't matter so much now. Everyone is happy how we all cleaned the canal together. We even are planning another shramadana."

In another village—and a poor one—the local people found it so rewarding to share a meal together in the course of their first shramadana that they decided to continue the practice. They proceeded to organize on their own a monthly Sunday "potluck," where families join to eat together the food they jointly contribute and prepare.

While caste in Buddhist Sri Lanka is far less complex and rigid than in Hindu society, from which it originally derives, it is still reflected in customs of marriage and, to a lesser extent, of commensality (eating together). As in any Asian society, the partaking of another's food is an expression of respect. In shramadanas, as in its preschools, community kitchens, and training centers, Sarvodaya's goal of social equality—as well as the Buddha's original teachings against caste—are expressed concretely through the common meals.

Collective provision of food also gives villagers useful organizational experience. Often it is the newly formed Sarvodaya Youth Committee that goes house-to-house to solicit donations. Their task is facilitated by the local Sarvodaya monk, who may accompany them or give them a letter to take around. The process itself provides them a double opportunity: to explain to families the nature of Sarvodaya and shramadana, and to learn from each family in turn about its situation and needs. Like all other activities preliminary to a camp, this food-canvassing offers immediate and invaluable experience in grassroots organizing.

SHARING IDEAS

The sharing of ideas is also integral to the shramadana experience thanks to the institution of *paule hamuas* or "family gatherings." These precede the camp, to discuss and plan its work, and then in the course of the camp are usually held three times a day. After the collective meals the participants meet "as a family" to organize the day's work teams and to do the ritual chants, prayers, and meditations. At the midday and evening meetings they discuss the project and other village needs, listen to talks, and entertain each other with song and dance. This takes time. A young monk-organizer I know thought it took too much time, wished he could dispense with the gatherings so that more yards of canal could be cleaned; but the value of these gatherings—in the eyes of the Movement and of this observer-participant—is evident. They play a key function in transmitting ideology, generating a sense of community, and providing a forum for discussion of village needs.

This is possible because the gatherings occur within the context of collective work. That context is basic to their effectiveness. Indeed, I came to believe that shramadana's distinctive contribution to grassroots development lies in the way it combines physical work with town meetings. These two poles of the work camp are in dynamic relationship, each informing and motivating the other. The prayers and speeches of the *paule hamua* give inspiration to tasks as mundane as digging latrines; they furnish concepts by which villagers can appropriate the meaning of the work and build from it a new self-image, new plans. For its part the labor itself makes the ideas immediate, tangible. It also empowers villagers to participate in the meetings, helping them feel they have earned the right to share their views. After a day's work alongside other community members, those who are customarily reluctant to express themselves, because they are poor or uneducated or young or women, are more disposed to speak up—and to be listened to. In Sri Lanka, Sarvodaya's family gatherings are notable for the role assumed by village women, young people, and children, learning to speak in public as if their ideas, too, were worth sharing. Participation in the family gatherings can be improved, for old habits of passivity persist; but even so they provide a forum for sharing ideas and discussing problems and plans that is hard to find elsewhere in rural Sri Lanka.

> Only in shramadana can you collect people like brothers under one roof, so they can talk and plan and build the spiritual man.
>
> *(District coordinator)*

> Seeing the *Paule Hamua* changed my life.
>
> *(Police inspector)*

To visiting government functionaries and politicians the shramadana offers a contact with village life that is often inspiring and always informative. Many are evidently moved not only by the voluntary and collective nature of the work, but also by the character of the meetings, reflecting as they do renewed vitality of their country's traditions. I saw on separate occasions an Assistant Government Agent (A.G.A.) and a Gram Sevaka stand to address the *paule hamua* and then proceed to deliver their remarks in extemporaneous sung verse, an ancient custom which has all but disappeared from Sri Lankan public life. They obviously enjoyed their audience's approval as well as relishing the challenge of intoning their speech in rhyme and meter.

> Like dawn's rays over the jackfruit trees
> so does this village illumine our life,
> as it broadens, like the Buddha's path
> of virtue, this road for wagons and jeeps....

"No," said the A.G.A. in response to my question, "I have not sung before in the course of official duties." Here again we see how the gap between the government and the rural population can narrow in the course of a shramadana, thanks to the organizing style and strategies of Sarvodaya.

Especially useful in bridging the gap is the exchange of information that can take place at a *paule hamua*. Some of the official guests' speeches are mundane exercises in rhetoric, but often they serve to explain government policies affecting the village and programs available to it. A District Health Officer tells the purpose of the inoculation program and how to use it. An Assistant Government Agent elucidates in simple terms the problem of deforestation, telling the villagers why it is in their long-term interest to observe current restrictions on cutting firewood and to learn which trees they should use. In return, when those presiding at the meeting are confident enough to encourage them (as I found more often the case with monks), villagers will express to the visiting officials their own views and questions. An old woman tells how local regulations have blocked her foodstamp book. A farmer describes the flooding and loss he suffered because of a public river-diversion scheme. In such ways does the shramadana serve to educate not only the villagers, but government personnel as well.

These family gatherings in the course of a camp are major social events in the village. The evening meetings especially—with their longer fare of song and dance (the villagers are given the opportunity to perform for each other) and their occasional showing of a Sarvodayan film—lure people with the entertainment they provide. Many come of an evening who did not take part in the day's work. Data collected by the Sarvodaya Research Institute show that a number of these, who are then exposed to the spirit and philosophy of Sarvodaya, return on subsequent days to labor on the project itself—and that these numbers tend to increase in the course of a shramadana.[4]

It should also be noted that participation in the meetings, by giving a speech or song, is encouraged by the equal treatment that each receives in response. Instead of extemporaneous applause, which would vary according to each offering (the more adept or influential persons winning more), the Sarvodaya practice is to respond each time with an identical, short, rhythmic round of claps. Whether to a Member of Parliament with resounding oratory, or to a child who stumbles over her words, the response is the same. Expressing the Buddha's teaching of *samanatmatha*, it confers equal dignity on all.

Family gatherings have a strong religious component, whether they take place in a temple setting or a preschool building or a make-shift shed near the worksite. If monks are on hand, they sit at the front facing the villagers and leading them in the opening meditation and chanting of the sacred verses. If the gathering includes non-Buddhist villagers or trainees, a hymn or invocation from their traditions is usually offered first. Without fail, even if clergy are not present, the verses (for the Triple Refuge, the Five Precepts, and often other sutras too) are chanted, and the two minutes' silence for meditation on lovingkindness (*metta*) is observed.

Less obviously religious, yet rooted in the Buddha's teachings, is the highly participatory nature and aim of these gatherings. In the earliest scriptural accounts of the meetings of the sangha (monastic community) as in the *Mahaparanibbanasutta* and the *Vinaya Pitaka*, practices of open debate and decision-making by consensus are described and advocated. These, consonant with the Buddha's anti-authoritarian posture and emphasis on self-reliance, have been heralded by political historians as the first recorded instances of democratic process.

THE USE OF SHARING LANGUAGE

Priyavachana (pleasant or kindly speech) is a traditional Buddhist concept that Sarvodaya has adopted and adapted for purposes of village awakening. Reflected in both the style and content of verbal communication, it promotes, in very simple ways, the sense of unity, dignity, and equality the Movement would generate. The use of kinship terms is almost *de rigueur* among the lay Sarvodayans, from regional directors to the newest village participant in a shramadana, with people of all rank and background addressed as "older brother," "younger brother," "older sister," "mother," etc.[5] Along with the avoidance of pejorative pronouns and verb forms that in the local

---

[4]Sarvodaya Research Institute, *Sarvodaya Study—Service in Sri Lanka 1975–1976.*
[5]The practice does not extend to the Movement's topmost level of leadership.

tongue reflect class and caste ranking, these modes of address serve to downplay the social distinctions and divisions that stratify traditional society.

> Call him *malli* [brother] and soon he begins to act like your brother. We've been divided against each other too long.
> (*Sarvodaya trainer*)

> She is a poor low-caste woman. She was surprised and happy when I, a graduate, called her *amma* [mother]. That alone teaches her some Sarvodaya philosophy.
> (*District coordinator*)

Kinship forms of address also serve to facilitate and make acceptable the intermingling of the sexes in Sarvodaya programs. Traditional villagers are often suspicious and disapproving of joint meetings and activities between young men and young women, and for that reason can be reluctant to allow their daughters to participate in a Sarvodaya Youth Group or shramadana. When the young people call each other brother and sister it helps to allay these fears—and also to keep flirting and other questionable behavior to a minimum, for the terms evoke for all an entire code of familial protection and respect.

The practice of *priyavachana* is also taken to mean that Sarvodayans speak to each other in mutually supportive ways, avoiding anger, criticism, or malicious gossip. These reflect the Buddha's emphasis on Right Speech, which not only condemns lying but specifies that verbal abuse, slander, and idle gossip are also unskillful and generative of bad karma. In a lengthy set of guidelines prepared by the Movement for the conduct of shramadana camps, almost half the items deal with interpersonal behavior. For example: If a person appears lazy or unreliable, do not scold him publicly. Do not ridicule him. Show by example; if the problem persists, discuss it with him. Do not refer to errors of the past; expect that he is discarding them. Do not talk of the misconduct of others. Do not repeat rumors. . . .

Although Sarvodayans complain about their own tendency to gossip, and talk behind people's backs, I found *priyavachana* observed more generally than I expected. Given my previous experience with people in groups, I was struck by the extent to which Sarvodaya workers appeared to expect the best from each other. Gentleness of behavior is, of course, a traditional ideal of Sri Lankan culture; what is new with Sarvodaya is the seriousness accorded it as a tool for village development.

DIFFICULTIES WITH SHRAMADANA

Sarvodaya's experience reveals not only the effectiveness of the shramadana method, but also the problems that can arise in using it. These also should be noted, as readers of this book and observers of the Movement consider its possible relevance to their own society. These problems, which are recognized by many organizers themselves, derive largely from the popularity that shramadana has gained in the Movement and the country, and from the ensuing need for better quality control. Over the years the method has spread so fast that it is sometimes undertaken with inadequately trained organizers, overly casual preparations, and superficial enlistment of support. Consequently it risks being misused, over-used, and trivialized.

A good shramadana does not just "happen"; for an organizer to help a village create that experience for itself requires skill, patience, experience, and understanding of Sarvodaya's philosophy. Shramadanas fall far short of their potential when their organizers are inadequately trained and assume that the process involves little more than assembling people and tools and putting up a Sarvodaya banner. As a veteran Sarvodayan said, "One well-organized shramadana is worth ten poor ones."

Both time and training often appear to be insufficient. Sometimes Sarvodayans rush to organize camps in order to complete a district quota ("I have to do five shramadanas in the next three weeks, so that we can put them on the district report.") When this occurs they give short shrift to the time that is necessary if the project is to be selected by consensus in village-wide meetings, if every household is to be canvassed and consulted, and if plans are to be coordinated with local schools and organizations, and government resources enlisted. Experienced organizers of successful shramadanas say that two months are required for adequate preparation, from the first steps until the work camp is ready to start. I have seen a large, excellent shramadana prepared in one month by a highly energetic and gifted monk, but any less time seems insufficient to lay the groundwork for the event.

Shramadana camps sometimes appear to be a group rather than a village undertaking; we see, for example, a band of several dozen young people making a community garden or compost pit while the community at large continues its daily activities as if oblivious of this collective effort. It seems easier to go ahead and do the job, than to try to enlist the energies and contributions of the rest of the village. Consequently the learning that is involved (learning about compost, say, as well as about one's own capacities for collaborative effort) is restricted.

Verbal participation in village "family gatherings" is sometimes limited to those Sarvodayans who have assumed the role of speaking and performing for the others. While these community meetings are more participative than other grassroots forums, they fall short of their own objective when they do not enable a good proportion of the villagers to move out of the passive role of spectator. This is not due to a failure of intention so much as to a lack of the time and tools that are necessary for an organizer to help village people speak up and share their views.

It is clear that the weaknesses just enumerated are not intrinsic to the method of shramadana; to some extent they appear a function of its very popularity and of the ensuing lack of time taken to organize it in a more thorough fashion. Even with these shortcomings in practice, it remains the Movement's most valuable contribution to grassroots development strategy, providing a model for recruiting and motivating the local population, inculcating leadership skills, and fostering the unity and initiative essential for self-help.

In these methods as in the Movement's goals, religious tradition serves as a resource for development. In the process, as elements relevant to contemporary social needs are brought to the fore, the tradition itself is reinvigorated.

V

The Monk in Community Development

ORANGE ROBES BRIGHTEN MANY A SARVODAYAN GATHERING, for an important resource that the Movement draws from religion is the participation of the clergy as village-level workers. While these clerics include Muslim mullahs, Christian pastors, and Hindu priests, most of them by far are Buddhist monks or *bhikkus*, given the predominant role of the Dharma in Sri Lanka and in Sarvodaya. It is, therefore, the Sangha (Order of Monks) whose function in community development we examine here.

Well over a thousand monks in their separate temples serve the Movement, many of them on what they consider a "full-time" basis. Depending on the extent of their clerical responsibilities (preaching, teaching, conducting ritual services, maintaining temple premises, etc.), this can mean anywhere from six to sixty hours a week. Given the resources of time, prestige, and education which the monks bring to this work, and given also the scope of this work—from convening a children's group to organizing a shramadana to interceding with government officials—the monks' contribution to the Movement's development program is substantial. Indeed, without this contribution Sarvodaya could hardly have spread so wide or penetrated so deep in Sri Lanka as it has.

The relationship between Sarvodaya and the Sangha is a symbiotic one, in that each benefits the other. As the monks serve as extension agents for the Movement's development program, so do the Movement's ideology and expectations serve to revitalize their Order and their sense of vocation, restoring the wider social responsibilities they carried in precolonial days. This effect on the Sangha is not incidental, or just a "spin-off," but an acknowledged goal of Sarvodaya, intrinsic to its interpretation of development as the awakening of *all*.

SARVODAYA'S BHIKKU PROGRAM

Monks are active at all levels of the Movement, working alongside their lay colleagues; fifteen serve on the fifty-one-member Executive Committee, one is a District Coordinator, many direct Gramodaya centers, while several thousand work full or part-time as grassroots community organizers. For mutual support and guidance they meet periodically in their own Sarvodaya Bhikku Association. This in turn is supported by the Movement's Bhikku Services, which also coordinate Sarvodaya training programs for monks. The most ambitious of these is the Community Leadership Training Institute for Bhikkus at Pathakada, built with German aid and offering residence for sixty monastic trainees and four-month courses in both Dharma and development.

The results of the Pathakada training institute have been disappointing, however; the courses are undersubscribed and many of its graduates do not continue in community development work. The reasons for this poor showing are rooted in the problems and hardships facing the Sangha in modern Sri Lanka.

The Sinhalese Sangha confronts problems of attrition and diminishing support. Joblessness and inflation erode the material sustenance that villagers can provide their monks, temples, and *pirivenas* (temple-sponsored schools). Fewer are joining the Sangha than before and, once enlisted, more are leaving it for remunerative employment. The monk who resists the lures of modern urban life, and remains to live and work in the local temple, finds himself with few or no colleagues to help with clerical duties. He cannot therefore take several months—or even a week or a few days—for training at Pathakada. By the same token, it is those monks who have assumed fewer village-level responsibilities who tend to come for a four-month Pathakada course. These include some who seek the training as a potential exit-visa from the Sangha and poverty, and who are, therefore, not greatly motivated for Sarvodaya development work as an end in itself. A 1977 study by the Sarvodaya Research Institute showed that 26.6% of the trainees continued on in community development, while 1980 estimates offered by the lay co-director of Bhikku Services indicate thirty to forty percent.

But these figures are not to be taken as a measure of Sarvodaya's bhikku work, for most monks active in the Movement are not Pathakada-trained. Many, unable to afford the time for extensive courses, engage in the Movement directly, acquiring the ideology and organizational skills "on the job" and in brief regional meetings sponsored by Bhikku Services.

DEVELOPMENT ACTIVITIES OF THE MONK

Interviewing scores of monks on the village scene, and observing these and many more of them at work, I was able to conclude that the role of the Sangha in Sarvodaya's grassroots development activities is extensive and significant. It is also unique. For in each of the main ways the monk serves the Movement—introducing it to the village, articulating its ideology, organizing its activities, mediating with the power elite—he brings the distinctive advantages and capacities with which his tradition endows him.

Introducing Sarvodaya

Monks function as a major channel through which Sarvodaya activities and personnel are introduced to a village. From his research into participation in Sarvodaya, Professor J. Lin Compton of Cornell University reports that the party credited most frequently by villagers as instrumental in "getting Sarvodaya started" is the local or visiting clergy. These were cited more than twice as often as the next category of local person, the schoolteacher.[1] As Compton points out, both monks and teachers, because of the more reflective nature of their occupations, are usually quicker to envisage the needs and the prospects for change than other village residents.[2]

In addition to being more likely to hear about Sarvodaya from professional colleagues, and more ready to see its promise for the local scene, monks also have the prestige in the eyes of the villagers to "sell" a new idea. To Compton's query as to who is "most important in giving legitimacy to Sarvodaya activities," villagers again cited the monks and almost twice as often as the second ranking category.[3] It is not difficult for the monk to spread the work because he is the local figure most frequently consulted by local people. When asked *where* they discussed their problems, most respondents by far said the temple, citing it more than twice as often as their home and almost four times as often as any other public place. When asked with *whom* they discussed their problems, villagers again ranked the clergy highest.[4]

These findings by Compton are confirmed by my own observations, as I repeatedly saw monks serve as the moving force in launching Sarvodaya activities. When it happens to be a lay person who brings the germ of the Sarvodaya idea, perhaps from attending a shramadana in another village, usually he or she will approach the monk first to get his support—and, hopefully, his active involvement—before attempt-

---

[1] J. L. Compton, *Participative Education Programming* (Cornell University, for U.S. A.I.D., Washington, D.C., 1970, unpublished), p. 155.
[2] *Ibid.*, p. 158.
[3] *Ibid.*, p. 255.
[4] *Ibid.*, p. 129.

ing to present it to other villagers. This is to be expected, not only because of the monk's prestige—useful in persuading people that the Movement is not politically partisan or insurrectionist—but also because social service activities in rural Sri Lanka have been traditionally temple-related.

Transmitting the Goals of Sarvodaya

Bhikkus also serve, far more than any other persons, to articulate to the villagers the nature and goals of Sarvodayan development. In answer to Compton's question as to who "has played instructional roles in Sarvodaya projects in your village," respondents placed the clergy first, twice as often as other village leaders or lay Sarvodayan organizers.[5]

The kinds of information conveyed by the monks can be concrete: where to dig clay for bricks, how to organize a marketing cooperative, how deep to excavate an irrigation canal, how to grow medicinal herbs, etc.; for Sarvodaya's bhikku program helps them to provide such technical assistance. The monks' main instructional role, however, is ideological, transmitting the Sarvodayan philosophy of development and grounding it in religious terms familiar to the people.

Buddhist scripture offers many apt and memorable illustrations of this philosophy. In the *Kutadanta* and *Agganna* and other sutras, for example, the Buddha stresses the necessity for local economic self-reliance and egalitarian sharing across the caste and class lines. Even more familiar to young and old are the Jatakas (birth-tales of the Buddha's earlier incarnations in animal and human form); like the tales of the rabbit, the elephant leader, or the king of the monkeys, these vividly portray the qualities of self-offering and compassion.

A favorite story is that of Magha, from the *Dhammapada-Katha*. One day, when he was still a man, Magha began voluntarily to clean up the litter that befouled his village's meeting-place. The results were so rewarding that he began to clear the road to the village, cutting back the overgrown foliage and removing rocks. When a passer-by asked what he was about, he answered, "I am treading the path to Nirvana"— whereupon the inquirer joined in the work. Each time they were questioned, the answer was the same, "We are treading the path to Nirvana"; and soon there were thirty-three of them laboring together. At the end Magha became Sakka, the King of the Gods in the realm of the thirty-three Gods. This, say Sarvodaya monks, is the story of the first shramadana.[6]

Sarvodaya's lay leadership, recognizing the value of this inspirational role, urges the monks not to neglect it in favor of technical and administrative aspects of the program, for these can be increasingly

---

[5]*Ibid.*, p. 219.
[6]Although voluntary collective labor was known in Ceylon, especially in pre-colonial times, the term *shramadana* and its modern practice date from the inception of the Sarvodaya Movement in 1958.

handled by the growing number of trained lay organizers. In the 1980 annual meeting of the Sarvodaya Bhikku Association, the clergy were told, "Remember, your chief work is to prepare *minds*," to help people "see their needs and to see they can work together to meet these needs." This is essential, for "the real revolution is in the mind."

Organizing Sarvodaya Projects

Sarvodaya monks, of course, do not limit their work to ideology; in many village settings they are the initiators and chief sustainers of Sarvodaya groups and activities. In Compton's survey locals were asked who was "instrumental in organizing Sarvodaya activities"; again the monks were cited most frequently—45% more often than the next highest category.[7]

The bhikku's work as community organizer is enhanced by the prestige and trust the villagers accord him and by his familiarity with local resources, both human and material. For the temple is the central nexus of the web of village life; and if anyone knows "what's going on," it is usually the monk. But his status and strategic location are not enough: he must get up and out.

> Don't sit in your temple like a rich monk waiting for dana. Go to the people, go to the poorest, work with them.
> *(Sarvodaya monk to his fellow bhikkus)*

Such venturing out can be at some personal cost, however, for a given village may be unfamiliar with this kind of clerical behavior.

> At first there was criticism in the village. Some people didn't like it, the way I was walking all around with the children and young people I got to help me.
> *(Sarvodaya monk)*

Monks are usually instrumental in organizing both shramadanas and Sarvodaya village committees of children, youth, mothers, farmers, and elders. The staging of the shramadana camp serves to catalyze these groups, with the youth committee usually taking the lead and in collecting food, tools, and people, with the monk acting as their mentor, and with the temple as their meeting place. During the camp itself, the monk often supervises the work. His presence, furthermore, serves to set the tone of the event, ensuring that rowdyism and conflict are avoided. Layfolk and clergy alike see this as important; they frequently emphasized to me that at Sarvodaya shramadanas, in contrast to other work camps, there is no fighting and drinking, and this is thanks to the bhikkus. Monks also use their organizational role here to further the social and ethical aims of the Movement:

> In setting up the work teams for the camp I took care to put people

---

[7]Compton, *ibid.*, p. 164.

from different castes and different ends of the village on the same
team. They did not wish to argue with me and I did not say anything,
but I knew it would start breaking the divisions between them.

(Sarvodaya monk)

The monk makes the temple available both as locus and catalyst
for Sarvodaya work. Customary rituals, such as evening *mal puja*, or
flower-offering to the Buddha, are often used by Sarvodaya bhikkus as
the occasion for prompting discussion among the villagers. The *bana
maduwo*, or preaching hall, makes an excellent site for village "family
gatherings". The spacious temple compound serves often as premises
for the newly organized Sarvodaya preschool, community kitchen,
and library, and even for batik workshops, medicinal gardens, and
masonry training programs. Here, in this venerable setting, the monk
can bring together the influential landowner and members of the new
Sarvodaya youth group, the rich merchant and the indigent farmer.

Out of these contacts and the groups they start, monks can organize wider-based, long-term projects having economic impact on the
village. Such bhikku-initiated projects with which I am personally
familiar include a local tea-marketing cooperative, a coconut cultivation cooperative, a fruit-tree nursery, a coir-processing plant and the
reclamation of marshland for a training farm. The monks also instigate
social service activities, from first aid and literacy classes to hospital
clean-up campaigns. Such accomplishments are not without cost to the
bhikku in time and comfort and material substance. Since Sinhalese
monks receive no clerical salary and depend on the alms of the faithful,
they often need an independent income to live without penury, especially in a poor village. I can name a number who have quietly, and
sometimes at a sacrifice, funded local Sarvodaya projects from their
own purses, or given family-owned land and materials. Similarly, I
know Sarvodaya monks who chose to leave the comfort and beauty of
a major vihara, and the amenities their age, status, and accomplishments earned them, to work as organizers among the poor. This has
meant going to backward areas where there was not even a rudi-
mentary temple, just a hut in a new "model village" or a makeshift,
open-walled structure on a hillside.

As village-level organizers, monks serve not only to initiate local
groups but also to provide continuity. This is especially significant in
relation to Sarvodaya youth and children's groups, whose membership
is by nature subject to high turnover. The bhikku, often the main adult
working with them, provides ballast—a maturity of judgment and
continuity of presence that these groups would not otherwise have. He
is also valuable, as we see below, in helping them present their purposes
and plans to the community at large.

Mediating with the Power Elite

Monks promote grassroots development by facilitating interactions between the villagers and those who hold political, administrative, or economic power in the area. This role is a valuable one, helping
to bridge the gap of mutual ignorance and suspicion that often
separates the village from those who can offer some of the needed
resources. Being a revered, nonpartisan, and relatively well-educated
figure, the motivated monk can play this role better than anyone else.

Often it is the bhikku who invites the government extension
agents and politicians to attend a shramadana, or who goes in person to
their offices or homes to inquire about the nature and availability of
government programs for his village. By virtue of his robes alone, he is
treated with deference.

> I always try to take a bhikku with me when I go to the A.G.A.'s
> office. That way I can get right into see him and not have to spend
> hours waiting.
>
> *(District-level organizer)*

Some of the most effective monk organizers I know are particularly adept at relating with local administrative or political personages;
trusted and respected by those in power, they can enlist their cooperation and repay it by providing them gratifying contact with the grassroots and a sense of virtue in seeing a project get off the ground.
However, Sarvodaya's president Ariyaratna cautions the monks
against becoming dependent on these power figures, or co-opted and
bedazzled by them. Speaking to the Sarvodaya Bhikku Association in
1980, he said: "Don't feel you must recruit the A.G.A. or curry favor
with the M.P. Just go to the people and work with them. That's where
the real power is."

The bhikku's value, Ariyaratna continued, lies in his independence: "Remember the politicians can get other folks transferred, but
they can't transfer *you*. The worst they could do is put you in jail, but
jail is made for people—you just continue your work there."

Sometimes the most dramatic gains for a village consist of access to
what is already available—as in the acquisition by one indigent village
of some fifty acres of sorely needed land. Appropriated by the government in the dismemberment of large estates in 1972, the land had not
been distributed to the local people—until a local Sarvodaya monk
successfully approached the officials. ("No one had gone to ask for it
before," he said.) In "asking," the monk also saw to it that the government supplied materials for the construction of fifty houses; these were
then built in a remarkable fifty-day shramadana camp that the monk
organized. The festivities at the project's conclusion celebrated in
addition a new access road, a coir factory, and a Sarvodaya preschool

where literacy classes and family gatherings now take place each evening.

Most monk organizers prefer that villagers go themselves to deal with officials, at least initially, for this gives them valuable experience and builds confidence. Since the disadvantaged are often timid, the bhikku gives them encouragement and suggestions as how to present their case. He also prods the women—it might be a Sarvodaya pre-school teacher, health worker, or head of the Mothers' group—to represent themselves directly in articulating their needs. He and they know that he is ready to step in if necessary to intercede on their behalf.

Because they have access to the more affluent and educated elements of the society, monks can, as we noted, encourage them to join in Sarvodaya work, or at least to support it. Employing no divisive political rhetoric, they can motivate the powerful while working with the powerless—and help both to collaborate.

Serving as Symbol of Tradition and Personal Commitment

Underlying all these ways that monks serve Sarvodaya's development goals, is the monks' value as a symbol. In each of these activities, his presence and engagement carry an added charge that distinguishes his contribution from that of a lay person doing the same thing. His robes and monastic discipline dramatize the continuity of tradition and development. They show that the betterment of life's material circumstances does not require dislocation from the country's age-old culture, but can draw from its meanings and resources.

Furthermore, his actions dramatize the personal commitment that is needed for national renewal. Instead of just receiving from the fruits of the economy (as he could legitimately do), the monk is seen *giving* to it of his time, energy, and substance. The sight of him meeting early and late with Sarvodaya youth or children, or going out in the sun to mark the road for the shramadana, has inspirational value, motivating villagers to engage more seriously and work harder themselves.

For this reason partly, Sarvodaya monks are also known to engage in the physical labor of a shramadana. As one of them remarked, "How can I expect the young people to work, if I just stand there under my umbrella?"

It is also the contagious spirit or the emotional "high" of a shramadana that prompts monks to depart from custom to this extent. Except for attending to personal needs and cleaning temple premises, manual work is traditionally considered unworthy of the Sri Lankan monk, especially activities—such as digging—which can destroy small living creatures. But monks at a shramadana have been known not only to pass buckets of excavated dirt, but also to help roll boulders and cut earth for a road which is, strictly speaking, against the rules. Opinions vary as to the severity of the offense: some monks tell me it depends on the motivation, others that it can only be absolved by subsequent confession. In any case, this departure from custom is more acceptable now than in the recent past. It reflects and symbolizes the concern for development that is spreading in the Sangha, a concern for which Sarvodaya itself is largely reponsible.

LAY-CLERGY PARTNERSHIP

In contrast to other cases of Sangha social service, monks who do development work with Sarvodaya engage themselves in a partnership with lay people on village, district, and national levels. This partnership offers distinct advantages—as well as challenges.

The Sangha's concern for the material welfare of the people obviously predates Sarvodaya. The annals of Ceylon's ancient history tell how the Order advised the rulers on the vast irrigation system that made the island the "Granary of the East," and supervised its construction and maintenance. Indeed, it was out of the earth excavated for canals and reservoirs (or "tanks") that the great religious stupas and temples were built. This close relation between religion and economic life—or between "temple and tank," as it is traditionally expressed—was fragmented by the colonial powers as they removed from the Sangha its educational and developmental roles. Individual monks who were so motivated continued in sporadic social-service activities, but it was not until Sarvodaya in our time that the Sangha engaged in community work in an organized fashion.

Those socially committed monks who have joined Sarvodaya after working independently, say they find benefit in the wider structure and support the Movement provides. One bhikku, for example, who had built a community center with health and educational services for the poor, joined Sarvodaya after twenty-five years of such work. He says he has found it a clear advantage to be able now to send his young lay-people for Sarvodaya training; they bring back skills and techniques that enrich the work, as well as subsistence allowances which permit some to engage in it on a more regular, full-time basis. At the same time the monk himself can share his own considerable experience more broadly at Sarvodaya meetings throughout his region and beyond.

Young lay co-workers undergird the bhikkus' efforts, extend their reach, and increase the flow of information. The significance of this teamwork is highlighted by its absence in a program like National Heritage, a 1970s attempt to launch a Buddhist rural development movement external to Sarvodaya. Its demise was partly due to its over-dependence on individual clergy and the lack of trained lay co-workers. Examples of Sangha-dependent development efforts can be found outside Sri Lanka, too. In Thailand, for example, Buddhist monks have a long tradition of community service, recently revitalized by special training programs (with support from external agencies such as the Ford Foundation). While these programs are useful, they are not structured to engage lay people and monks together, as Sarvodaya does. Thai monks working in development lack the psychological support and stimulus of lay colleagues engaged in the same venture, as well as the multiplier effect that local, full-time lay co-workers could provide.

As the Co-Director of Sarvodaya's Bhikku Services notes, this is the first time in Sri Lankan history that monks have worked within a lay organization, side by side with lay colleagues. It is not surprising, therefore, that tensions and difficulties occasionally arise, especially in the exercise of authority and supervision. This was not a problem before Sarvodaya's decentralization, when issues could be resolved at Headquarters level by a joint committee of lay and monk elders. But now individual monks find their Sarvodaya activities subject to the authority of lay district coordinators. At a meeting of the Sarvodaya Bhikku Association, some complained that decisions affecting their village work are made without consulting them, and others acknowledged that they found it awkward and even demeaning to have that work subjected to criticism by young district-level organizers. To avoid such difficulties, the Sarvodaya Bhikku Association is exploring special measures for the supervision of monks' work, measures that are consonant with decentralization.

These development activities of the monks have a profound effect, not only on the villagers but on the Sangha itself. They affect its self-image and its understanding of the Dharma—and in ways that are highly relevant to a people's capacity for self-help. By drawing on the resources of religion, Sarvodaya has expanded those resources.

VI

Expanding the Resources of Religion for Development

I N THE TOWN OF RATNAPURA IN AUGUST 1981 AN UNPRECEDENTED
event took place. Along with vast crowds of community development organizers, five thousand Buddhist monks assembled and
moved in processions which included all three of the Nikayas or sects
that traditionally have divided the Sinhalese Sangha. On the flower-
decked platform, leading the chanting of sacred sutras, were the heads
of these sects, sitting together for the first time in history. The occasion
was the funeral of the Venerable H. Gnanaseeha, the monk-scholar who
had directed Sarvodaya's training program for bhikkus. The extraordi-
nary unity and vitality of the event stemmed from Sarvodaya's work in
establishing the relevance of religion in the modern world.

When the Sarvodaya Movement had its birth in 1958, with a high-
school work camp in an outcaste village, Ariyaratna, its leader, did not
find a religious establishment ready and primed to engage in community development, nor did prevalent notions of Buddhist piety embrace
such a commitment. It was only as he and his colleagues listened to the
villagers and understood their belief-systems that this happened. It was
as Ariyaratna drew on his own considerable Buddhist scholarship, as
he found kindred spirits among the monks, and as he provided them
opportunities to serve, that the Sangha began to reclaim its broader
role in society—and a broader understanding of the import of the
Buddha's teachings. The process has fostered within the enlarged
society a renewed understanding of the role of the Sangha, the meaning
of the Dharma, and the significance of personal spiritual practice.

In other words, as Ariyaratna drew on the resources of religion for
development, these resources expanded. This reciprocal dynamic takes
place in other faith-systems as well, as we can see from the work of

Gandhi or Catholic worker-priests, or from Sarvodaya's own work in Hindu, Muslim, and Christian communities. Taking the case of the Movement's engagement with the Dharma, let us see its effects on that tradition.

RECONSTRUCTING RELIGIOUS VOCATION

In 1979 and 1980 I noted that the Sangha's attitudes toward development work had shifted somewhat since my previous visit to Sri Lanka in 1976. At that time questions were still raised, among more conservative monks, about the legitimacy and appropriateness of engaging in community development activities; but three and four years later such doubts were no longer expressed to me. If suspicions persist about the propriety of bhikku village work, they are not communicated openly. This is partly because such work is now seen as distinct from political activity; Sarvodaya has offered to monks an arena for engagement that does not embroil them in the partisan politics which in earlier years had brought criticism to the Sangha and dispute within it. Community development now seems accepted as a pursuit worthy of a monk. It is still, however, not as highly regarded by the population as a monk's withdrawal to "the forest" for meditation and the pursuit of enlightenment.

Some Sarvodaya monks still reflect ruefully on the relative lack of esteem accorded to socially active bhikkus (in contrast to "forest dwelling" monks), but meanwhile they and senior clergy like the late Ven. Gnanaseeha, are altering the very conceptual basis on which such judgments are made. They are reconstructing the monastic vocation to give greater validation to compassionate activity in society. The ideal of the Bodhisattva, which historically has been more popular in Mahayana Buddhism than in Sri Lanka's Theravada tradition, is increasingly evoked. This figure personifies action for others, and a willingness to postpone enlightenment for the sake of others, rather than withdrawal from society to pursue his own release from suffering.

> I do not aim now for that release, or even to become a stream-winner[1]—at least not for many lives. There is too much work to do to help my fellow-beings out of poverty, greed, ignorance. I am ready to wait till everyone can enter nirvana with me. It will take a while.
>
> *(Sarvodaya monk)*

Some monks in the Movement even argue that identification with the needs of others does not represent a postponement of enlightenment so much as a different *means* of ultimately realizing that freedom from the bonds and delusions of the ego.

---

[1] "Stream-winner", in Buddhist belief, is one of the final stages of spiritual development, preliminary to ultimate release from the realm of suffering.

These monks bestow a new meaning on the traditional and preeminent virtue of *detachment*. Frequently in the past this ideal of Buddhist behavior has been equated with withdrawal from the world and indifference to the ebb and flow of human affairs. Now a different notion of detachment emerges. Instead of aloofness from social concerns, Sarvodayan monks see it as representing the freedom to act—i.e., the detachment from family responsibilities and job pressures—that makes the bhikku, in their eyes, the "natural" community development worker, one who can devote his full energies to village awakening.

REINTERPRETING DOCTRINE

By the very process of drawing inspiration from Buddhist teachings, Sarvodaya's efforts cast a fresh light on them, one that brings into bold relief the social content and implications of the Dharma. Like forms of "liberation theology" in contemporary Christianity, this perspective represents not so much a departure from tradition as a return to the early teachings of its founder and a reclamation of their original meaning. These teachings become, once again, "revolutionary"—as Ariyaratna recognizes:

> We believe that Buddhist teaching devoid of this revolutionary meaning and application is incapable of facing the realities of modern materialistic society.[2]

As we saw in Chapter III, the Buddha's views on caste and economic and political life have been reemphasized by the Movement to support its efforts toward social equality, local self-reliance, and participation in decision-making. Similarly Sarvodaya has retrieved the Buddha's original teaching on karma, distinguishing it from a fatalistic acceptance of predestination and presenting it as the operation of volition—hence a summons to act.

> Karma is not fate. It is one's own doing which reacts on one's own self, and so it is possible to divert the course of our lives...(Once we understand that) inactivity or lethargy suddenly transforms itself into activity leading to social and economic development.[3]

Meanwhile, as we have seen, the Four Noble Truths themselves have been reconceptualized. Recast in social terms, they show that the dependent co-arising of suffering—and hence the possibility of transcending it—applies on the collective as well as the individual level.

Some senior Sarvodaya monks, including the late Ven. Gnanaseeha, had their hand in this revision of the teachings, but it would not have occurred in so bold and systematic a fashion if Ariyaratna himself

[2]Ariyaratna, *Collected Works I*, p. 132.
[3]_____, *In Search of Development*, pp. 15, 28.

had not been deeply versed in the Dharma. His Buddhist scholarship, which was acquired early—for he spent much of his childhood in the company of the learned monks near his village home—is remarkable for a lay person, especially one who has devoted himself to public life.

RENEWING THE PRACTICE OF MEDITATION

Another new development in Sri Lankan Buddhism, which Sarvodaya fosters without fanfare, is the wedding of meditation and social action. Traditionally these two aspects of Buddhist life have been polarized—not only in the populace, but within the Sangha itself, with monks expected to choose between the *ganthadhura* (contributing to society through learning and teaching and healing) and the *vipassana-dhura* (the solitary, meditative path). Sarvodaya, by incorporating meditation in its meetings and holding optional meditation courses for its staff, bridges or combines these two pursuits.

The practice of meditation underwent a long period of drought; a century ago, for example, the great Buddhist reformer Dharmapala was hard put to find a meditation teacher on the island. But in the last generation, meditation practice has been reinvigorated for laity and clergy alike, in Sri Lanka as well as in other Buddhist countries. What Sarvodaya is doing is merging meditation with social responsibility, encouraging cultivation of the centered mind to breed both motivation and staying power.

Different types of meditation serve different uses for social action, as a Sarvodaya monk explained to me. The practice of *metta* (lovingkindness), which is the type most widely used in the Movement, releases the energy of compassion. *Samadhi* (one-pointed contemplation) develops endurance, and *vipassana* (mindfulness or insight meditation) helps take one beyond ego to freedom and fearlessness, enabling action-for-others to flow more easily.

Ariyaratna sees meditation as necessary not just to strengthen the individual, but to cleanse the mental and moral environment as well. It is not only our physical atmosphere which becomes polluted, he says; the "psychosphere" in which we live is poisoned by power struggles, by greed and fear and hatred, and these thoughts and impulses choke the community on a subconscious level. To dispel this pollution Sarvodayans must generate positive healing energy with the full force of their focused intention. Twice a day, on rising and before sleep, they are, as Ariyaratna tells them, to collect their dispersed thoughts through *anapanasati*, breath meditation. Then the energy thus concentrated is to be disseminated for the good of all beings through the *metta*, lovingkindness meditation. The third step, called both *prarthana* and *adhitthana*, consists of a conscious willing, whereby "the purified thought-force is directed toward the goal of a morally righteous and materially contented society." In Sarvodaya this directed intention frequently takes the form of an ancient Ceylonese invocation, which is chanted at "family gatherings":

> May there be rain enough.
> May there be prosperity.
> May the whole world be happy.
> May the rulers be righteous.

Non-Buddhists as well as Buddhists join in the chanting as they do in the meditations, for neither is dependent on any creed.

Some Sarvodaya monks meditate very little if at all—or rather, when asked, say that they find their "meditation objects" in the acts of social service. The very pressures of this work can then seem to force a blending or convergence of the two once-separate paths.

> People come more and more with their problems, even when I am busy or tired. So I just wash my face and meditate a few minutes. Then I can speak to help them see more clearly, and take their worries so they will be lightened.
>
> (*Sarvodaya monk*)

So we see meditation and social action interact in ways that empower each other; the dynamic is similar to that between the Dharma itself and the social economy—or between "temple and tank." In this dynamic interaction both change. Sarvodayans believe they are not altering religious tradition so much as returning it to its former role in their country's development. But by virtue of becoming relevant to today's needs, the tradition itself changes—which is true of all systems that are alive.

VII

Religion and Women in Development

RECENT YEARS HAVE BROUGHT INCREASING RECOGNITION OF THE importance of women to development. The inadequacy of developmental approaches and strategies that overlook women's historic role and potential contribution has also become apparent. Whether or not women "hold up half the sky," as the Chinese saying goes, they certainly preserve a major portion of the ground on which the country's health and strength depend, especially in terms of human nurture, including provision and preservation of food and the other necessities they produce on a noncash basis in Third World societies. Recent studies in world development show how modernization has eroded women's traditional roles, while increasing their burdens, and how the prevailing economic approach to development does not effectively integrate their energies.[1]

Sarvodaya is notable for its capacity to engage the participation of rural women. Although it functions in a patriarchal society, where women have been traditionally discouraged from playing a public role in community affairs, the Movement has succeeded in giving women a prominent role in the "awakening" of their villages. Indeed, on the grassroots level, more women than men participate in Sarvodaya—and not just as silent partners, but as active organizers and spokespersons. For many it is their first venture into responsibilities beyond home and family. As a Tamil village woman said, in regard to the Movement's impact on herself, her teenage daughter, and her sisters and neighbors, "Owing to this revolution, all these things that were shut in the houses are now coming out."

It is appropriate to consider this phenomenon within the context of our topic, the role of religion in development; for it is Sarvodaya's

[1]See I. Tinker and M. B. Bransen, eds. *Women and World Development*, Overseas Development Council, 1976.

creative relationship with religion that is largely the basis. Religion serves both to attract and to validate women's participation in Sarvodaya's activities. It draws on their traditional supportive role relative to temple and church; at the same time, it offers justification and protection from criticism, as they exceed this role and move out in fresh ways into their communities.

FEMALE PARTICIPATION IN SARVODAYA

In 1979 the Sarvodaya Research Institute undertook research on the role of women in Sarvodaya.[2] Its eight-month pilot study (in eleven villages by a two-woman team) revealed that in the Movement's grassroots programs women exceed men, and that these women tend to come from the more educated elements of the poorer strata of rural society. They are disadvantaged economically but not educationally, with about half having reached the 0 Level (eleventh grade) and only two percent unschooled. For most of them Sarvodaya is their first organization.

Village women's predominant involvement with the Movement is through the local Sarvodaya preschool, the Mothers' Group, and the Youth Group. The first two are closely linked, because when a woman puts a child in the preschool she automatically becomes a member of the *Mau Haule* (Mothers' Group). This in turn serves to engage her in broader health and nutritional concerns, thanks to the community kitchen that is often established in conjunction with the preschool, and to related health projects undertaken by the Sarvodaya-trained preschool teacher. The researchers also found in their preliminary study that females tend to engage more actively in the Youth Groups than do males, especially where these groups undertake projects focusing on health, educational, cultural, and moral concerns.

Village women also engage in Sarvodaya's shramadana camps. Like the Youth Groups, these provide for many their first opportunity to work with men outside their extended family circle. They also offer the excitement and challenge of undertaking physical labor on equal terms with men, and the sense of empowerment it brings. For many it is their introduction to the Movement. Although the practice of shramadana has been imitated by many organizations and agencies, from Rural Development Societies to the Mahaweli Irrigation Scheme, only Sarvodaya's work camps engage women to such a degree. Most non-Sarvodaya shramadanas are either closed to women or unattractive to them because of the kinds of behavior they tend to release. When undertaken without Sarvodaya's moral code and presence of clergy, they can lapse into drinking, gambling, fighting, and rowdy

[2]Unpublished. The researchers shared their findings with me personally.

conduct—which, of course, raises fears for the women who might attend them and suspicion upon those who do.

The sense of self-reliance and power that shramadana brings to women can be seen, sometimes dramatically, in subsequent actions they undertake. In the Jaffna peninsula, for example, local Sarvo-dayans held a work camp in 1974 to build a bund road—a sort of em-bankment—between the sea marshes and the land. The severe cyclone of 1978 demolished a section of this road, leaving a village inaccessible by wheel. It was the local Tamil women themselves, traditionally even more restricted to hearth and home than Sinhalese women, who decided to restore the bund by a shramadana of their own—and they did, organizing themselves into daily work battalions of four to five hundred females at a time. Within a month the road was ready for heavy vehicles.

Sarvodaya's meetings, from Mothers' Groups to community "family gatherings," give women the opportunity to speak up and share their experience and ideas. They are expected to express them-selves, even though this has not been the cultural norm, and many ini-tially feel painfully shy. For most it is their first exercise in public speaking. The researchers on the pilot study found a dramatic differ-ence in the participation of women between Sarvodaya and non-Sarvodaya meetings. They explain this in terms of the Movement's democratic and nonpartisan character: in other organizations the office-bearers are those who already have power in the village, whereas in Sarvodaya the poor and humble can come forward if they have the wits and motivation. The researchers came to believe that rural women can develop leadership skills to a greater degree in Sarvodaya than in any other situation.

The leadership that women exert in Sarvodaya is more evident on the grassroots level than in the Movement's district centers and national headquarters. Women constitute ten percent of the national Executive Committee and Elders' Council, and only one of the twenty-eight District Coordinators—proportions which are hardly representa-tive of the role they play in Sarvodaya programs. Even on the Gramo-daya (village awakening) level their responsibilities are usually placed under the direction of males. I encountered less sense of injustice in this arrangement than one would expect.

> Women do not resent this, because they know they lead in all the children's and health work, and much of the Youth Group work . . . and the men, on the district and national level, are just the adminis-trative heads.
>
> (Sarvodaya researcher, female)

In addition to the traditional female orientation of much of their

Sarvodaya work—in Mothers' Groups, preschools, community kitchens, crafts—women in the Movement also engage in activities and develop skills that are relatively new for them. Most of these relate to community-organizing, a type of work they had rarely seen modeled by women, and for which many initially felt they lacked the ability. I often asked them, "What do women do in Sarvodaya that they have not done before?" Replies ranged from public speaking to dealing with government officials and preparing programs and budgets.

In the Leadership Training courses offered at headquarters and district centers females are increasingly numerous, and are expected to perform as well as the males. Sarvodaya's trust in the effectiveness of women as organizers is based on the Movement's long experience with its preschool teachers, for child care and training are only a portion of these young women's responsibilities. The preschool teacher is often the first full-time Sarvodaya worker in a village, and as such she is frequently the avenue for subsequent activity. This means that in addition to recruiting the children, running the school and kitchen, engaging the mothers, and providing instruction on health, hygiene, and nutrition, she in many cases also initiates a Youth Group, instigates shramadana, deals with village leaders, extension agents, and monks, and, above all, transmits the philosophy and purposes of Sarvodaya. These functions take energy and also courage, for they entail actions that have not been customary for females and are therefore open to criticism and misunderstanding.

> So I went from house to house to tell people about the shramadana, even to low-caste families, like the potters. And our meetings to plan the shramadana often lasted till midnight. My family said that was unbecoming behavior for a woman, to be out at night and with such people.
>
> (*Sarvodaya preschool trainer*)

The broader leadership skills developed by preschool teachers have been increasingly recognized by Sarvodaya Headquarters. As the Movement has decentralized its operations, it has asked many of these young women to assume wider responsibilities, accepting more formally the community organizing duties they were already carrying out.

THE ROLE OF RELIGION IN FOSTERING FEMALE PARTICIPATION

Sarvodaya's goal of personality-awakening finds a ready response among women, especially as it is taken to mean the "building of a new person" from the infant up and the enlisting of young people in community service. In addition, religion serves to attract and sustain the participation of women in Sarvodaya in a number of specific ways.

Temple and Ritual Activities

Throughout Ceylonese history, as in traditional Western socie-ties, women have been closely associated with the local religious insti-tution—attending its rituals, supporting its clergy, and helping to beautify and maintain its precincts. In rural Sri Lankan Buddhism, in particular, female devotees have played a large and enjoyable role in temple life. Sarvodaya's religious flavor draws these women. Its early meetings are usually held in the preaching hall, often in conjunction with the evening's *mal puja* (flower offering to the Buddha). Its initial organizing projects frequently involve a shramadana to repair the temple. But even the Movement's activities do not take place in a religious setting, a religious flavor is present, both in Sarvodaya's philosophy and language and in its readiness to incorporate rituals. *Sil* campaigns (full-moon day observance), *peraheras* (religious parades with music and dance), and the mounting of the great *pandals* (decora-tive palm-leaf arches) all become incorporated into the activities of the Sarvodaya groups, along with their projects for village development, the latrines and gardens, preschool, and crafts.

Nonpartisan Personal Relationships

Many rural women are fearful of involvement with organizations because of the partisan conflict these tend to breed within the commu-nity. Most local societies and programs become identified with a given party, serving as vehicles for its interests and patronage, and as an arena for the petty politics that are far more divisive in the village than caste. The reluctance felt by many women to engage in this—combined with fear of adopting a partisan stand that could bring disadvantage in future political change—is abetted by their husbands, who for the same reason discourage them from joining. Sarvodaya, however, is seen as distinctively, even uniquely, nonpartisan (see Chapter III). The pilot study researchers stressed this factor as a crucial one in explaining the high participation of rural women in the Movement.

The Movement offers not only a nonpartisan arena for communi-ty action, but one, furthermore, which appears to foster more harmo-nious and trustful relationships than are found in other contexts. Sarvodaya women experience this solidarity not only with other females, but also with the men in the Movement. As a youth group member observed, "Sarvodaya men are closer to women than other men. They are friendlier, and also more respectful of us." The Sinhalese researchers on the pilot study were so struck by the kind of relationships between men and women that they saw in the Movement that they started its practice of *priyavachana* (in the use of kinship terms) among their fellow graduate students at the University. "It makes a difference, calling each other brother and sister, and it is catching on with some of the fellows. It gives a good "family feeling."

This family feeling, along with the Movement's assumption that each person can develop more fully, breeds a fraternal familiarity that can be expressed quite bluntly. I heard young male organizers scold their Sarvodaya "sisters" for hanging back in the traditional posture of modest timidity and not speaking out more boldly in meetings:

> Stop acting as if you didn't know what you want. Speak up. Don't whisper.

> Go on. You can do it by yourself. You organized most of the shramadana, you can go invite the A.G.A.

In the many Sarvodaya village meetings that I frequented, the men seemed supportive of the women's efforts, pleased when they took the initiative and ready to listen to their ideas. Indeed, in one District Center I knew, the young women had become more adept at leading the "family gatherings" and saw to it that the young male trainees, fresh from the villages, followed their example and learned how to speak and perform in front of others.

The very fact that young men and women work together in Sarvodaya is one of its attractions among rural youth. The high attendance at shramadanas is, in some degree, a function of the pleasure and excitement found in this—for the work camp, like the Youth Group, is a safe and respectable place where girls and boys can meet and get to know each other. From month to month, in different village shramadanas in the area, they can encounter again and enjoy each others' company, preparing meals, swapping tools, and concocting plans for future projects.

The Protective and Legitimizing Presence of Clergy

Young women in rural Sri Lanka are traditionally expected to stay close to home (even sometimes in the house), where their virginity and reputation can remain intact. For this reason many families are initially reluctant to permit their daughters to attend shramadana camps or participate in Sarvodaya's mixed Youth Groups. Again and again, as I observed, it is the presence of the clergy at these camps and meetings that makes the difference, reassuring parents that it is safe and respectable for their daughters, nieces, or sisters to join in. Often Sarvodaya monks go personally to the families to persuade them to give permission.

Sarvodaya clergy play the same legitimizing role in regard to the work of the female community organizer. Her task requires exposure and mobility in the village and the surrounding area; she is highly visible, walking about on her own, calling on low-caste households, going to meetings at night. The rumors and criticism this engenders can be considerable, when her motives and character are called into question by conservative relatives, usually older women. The local Sarvodaya monk comes to the rescue: he explains and praises the girl's work, lending his prestige to validate her efforts.

> People said it was not proper for a young woman to go about like that. But then the venerable monk accompanied me for a while, and the scolding and gossiping stopped.
>
> (*Sarvodaya organizer*)

Moral Effect on Village Behavior

One of the results of Sarvodaya activities in the villages, which is not touted in the Movement's literature or considered in development studies, is their effect on behavioral problems—especially drinking and gambling. In this period of cultural change and economic deprivation, where old securities and traditions weaken, drinking and gambling frequently become more severe, and the ensuing fights and feuding further sap village resources. These are major concerns of rural women. For Sarvodaya, village awakening means also the elimination of such conduct—seeing it as degenerative and supplanting it with self-discipline and constructive activity.

In more than one village with which I was familiar, alcoholic consumption had become a major problem among the men, draining their families' meager funds and triggering abuse of wives and children; but after a shramadana and the Sarvodaya activities generated, drinking was virtually wiped out. In one village, in the course of a month-long shramadana, most of the males decided to stop consuming arrack and toddy. Soon only one inveterate drinker remained; but because he was not acceptable in the evening family gatherings and classes that continued to take place, he eventually gave in, delivering to the young Sarvodaya resident worker a note written in his own blood: "Now I say I drink no more. There are better things for me to do in _____ [name of village]."

In some cases Sarvodaya children have a noticeable effect on their fathers' drinking habits. A veteran monk-organizer in the Movement considers this one of the chief rewards of his work with the *Singiti Haula* (Childrens' Groups). He describes instances of how money-saving schemes that the children are urged to start have inspired (or shamed) the fathers to check the flow of rupees into liquor, and of how the household devotions the children institute also shame the father when he comes home drunk, and help him "wake up" to his own behavior. Whatever the channels and means it uses, Sarvodaya's effect on patterns of drinking and gambling is a factor in the allegiance the Movement wins among rural women.

Dignity Accorded Traditional Work Roles

The modernization of developing rural societies often works to the disadvantage of women. As the cash economy invades the villages, women's traditional unpaid work is deprived of dignity and value. At the same time their work burden is increased, as they assume labors performed by male family members who seek remunerative employment elsewhere. In today's Sri Lanka the problems are compounded by the fact that many young village women are being drawn to the jobs offered in the industrialized free-trade or Investment Promotion Zones. Lured there by wages that turn out to be barely sufficient to cover the costs of food and lodging, they find the "profit" they gain in uprooting their lives is hardly enough for bus fare on occasional visits home.

Sarvodaya's efforts to generate income-producing projects for village women have met with uneven results. But even so its philosophy of rural economic development is one which restores dignity to these women's lives and work. This is because, by drawing inspiration from religious teachings, it accords value to all constructive work, and sees unpaid labor as a gift (*dana*) to society. The Movement functions, thereby, to breach the dichotomy between the formal and the non-formal (or cash and voluntary) sectors of the economy. By so doing it serves to enhance, rather than erode, the value perceived in the village roles of women.

Considerations of Family Planning

Sarvodaya's reluctance to sponsor family planning programs can be seen, as it is by some local and foreign observers, as detrimental to the status of women. For the Movement does not actively help them find release from the burden of unplanned children and overlarge families. Since Sarvodaya's leadership is not directly supportive of family planning (it is radically opposed to abortion, and unenthusiastic about contraception), its village-level workers do not usually assume a role in population control beyond referring people, when they ask, to local health officers and agencies. It is to be noted, however, that Sarvodaya headquarters facilities have been made available for training of government-sponsored family planning teams, and its organizing methods shared with them.

It is hard to tell the degree to which women may be alienated from Sarvodaya's development programs by its relative passivity in dispensing family planning information and its occasional (depending on the local organizers) opposition to the whole idea. On the one hand, other agencies and avenues exist for family planning in Sri Lanka, and Sarvodaya organizers can and do direct villagers to them. On the other, it should be remembered that in many rural areas the Movement is already breaking ground by bringing young men and women together as working colleagues. Among more conservative village elements, this mixing raises uncertainties and suspicions which would be all the greater if Sarvodaya were to peddle contraceptives at the same time.

There appears, however, no intrinsic reason why family planning could not be justified within the context of Sarvodaya philosophy. From the perspective of the Dharma, it is abortion and not contraception that is out of the question (one's incarnation as a conscious being begins with conception). While Sarvodaya leaders and monks say that self-control should make contraceptives unnecessary, a case could also be made for the compassion entailed in limiting unwanted births and keeping the population from exceeding its physical resources. But given the present tenor and leadership of the Movement, such a rationalizing effort may be too disruptive to be worthwhile, especially since other agencies have taken this mandate upon themselves.

RELIGION AND THE EMERGENCE OF WOMEN

Sarvodaya in its relationship to religion can be viewed as generating an Asian Buddhist form of "social gospel", a parallel to "liberation theology" in the West. As has occurred in regard to the teachings of Jesus, the Buddha's teachings on social equality, economic sharing, and political participation are being brought to the fore as a challenge — to inspire not just the enlightenment of individuals but the transformation of society itself.

Part of the challenge and travail of our time is the emergence of women. Seeking fulfillment, dignity, and responsibility, they emerge or "awaken" from over two millennia of patriarchy—a long era which set its hierarchical stamp on the religious as well as on the economic and political institutions of society, and during which the Sangha, like the Christian church, became male-dominated in both thought and practice. Given the patriarchal character thus imposed on religious traditions, one would expect emerging women to look elsewhere for support. But like those who are committed to social justice, their effort, too, seeks authentication in religion. Indeed, these two concerns—for justice in society and female participation in society— blend. And we see that it is those parties who assert the social relevance of a given faith system who also claim roles of responsibility for women. As the barriers that divided religion from society, meditation from action, or monks from economic development are increasingly breached, so are the bounds and strictures that relegated women to a lesser status. The Dharma offers resources for this emergence of women that Sarvodaya has only begun to tap, for women played a highly significant role in early Buddhist history, not only as the first female monastics, but as patrons and queens essential to the religion's survival.

It is not surprising, therefore, that the revitalization of the Buddhist social ethic brings with it an increased openness to the role of women. Historical and scriptural evidence is brought out, even in the popular press in Sri Lanka, to affirm the dignity and equality that women enjoyed in early Buddhist history, and the major role they played as saints, nuns, patrons, and scholars. While most of the more traditional clergy remain patriarchal, if not misogynist in their assumptions about women, it is those, I found, that are active and committed to community work who espouse a broader social role for women and exhort them to take greater leadership. A veteran Sarvodaya monk declared:

> During the long colonial period, women lost faith in themselves, became passive and preoccupied with narrow interests. Now they must reawaken to their central role in society. That means more than preschools, community kitchens, and crafts. They must take the lead now and be mentors to their villages in every respect. They are the key to the awakening of Lanka.

Because "modesty and shame" have become over the centuries the qualities prized in rural Sri Lankan females, this monk, like other bhikkus who promote a greater role for women, has to resort to telling them in a rather firm manner: "Get up and out. Plan the meeting yourselves." Meanwhile there are a growing number of Sarvodaya women organizers who do not need to be told.

> There are more leadership opportunities for women in Sarvodaya than elsewhere, and more women are joining. What it all amounts to is the resurgence of the ancient role of the mothers.
> *(Preschool-teacher trainer)*

This sense of the potential of female energy is reflected even in Sarvodaya's bhikku program, which includes among its activities a campaign to assist women who have taken the robes. The Order of Nuns disappeared from Ceylon centuries back, and since the male Sangha is generally loathe to reestablish it, the only monastic vocation open to women is that of *Dasasilmatha* (Ten-Vow Mother). Support, cloisters, schooling, and even much respect for these shaven and saffron-robed women are hard to come by; but Sarvodaya has made efforts to help them meet these needs and to organize them in service to community development. Because of an almost total lack of funds, such efforts are not conspicuously successful so far, but they are genuine. And they testify to a belief in the mutually-enhancing connections that exist between the Dharma and development and between development and women.

VIII

Lessons in Awakening: The Broader Relevance of the Sarvodaya Experience

W E HAVE SEEN THE GROWTH OF SARVODAYA FROM A HIGH-school holiday work camp to a people's self-help movement linking over four thousand villages. We have seen how it has drawn from religion to formulate goals for development, to make these goals meaningful to the people, and to develop strategies for collective action—strategies which also permit women, youth, and clergy to move beyond their customary roles in society and provide community leadership. All this is interesting enough in its own right, but does it have relevance beyond Sri Lankan shores? Does Sarvodaya's use of indigenous religious tradition offer lessons applicable to non-Buddhist societies? to industrialized as well as to developing countries?

These questions formed the theme of the founding conference of Sarvodaya Shramadana International, held in the Netherlands in May 1981 and attended by friends and followers of the Movement from six-teen countries around the world. Thanks to NOVIB, the semi-private Dutch foreign-aid agency active in Sri Lanka, many groups and fami-lies in Holland feel a strong connection with that former Dutch colony[1], and with the Sarvodaya Movement itself; they offered hospi-tality as development theorists and community organizers gathered from both industrialized and Third World countries. There in the Dutch town of Enschede, the "haves" and "have-nots" met in a spirit of mutual support as they explored together the broader relevance of Sarvodaya for our world today.

It was an assumption common to all participants that a new devel-opmental philosophy is essential in our time, for the industrialized countries can no longer serve as models of development. Their growth-oriented policies and high consumption levels deplete the planet's

[1]After about 150 years under Portuguese domination Ceylon was a colony of the Netherlands from 1658 to 1796. This period was followed by a century and a half under British rule.

resources, while polarizing the rich and the poor. In addition to the woes of inflation and unemployment, their pollution of the biosphere and their rising production, sales, and deployment of armaments now render questionable, for the first time in history, the very survival of the human species. Meanwhile, as the conferees pointed out, the industrialized societies themselves exhibit signs of acute social disorder and psychic alienation. In the face of the rigid, unresponsive bureaucracies of big business and big government, people feel anonymous and impotent to alter the drift of events. Indeed, a sense of personal powerlessness appears to be the feature most common to people in both "have" and "have-not" nations. It was in this context that the conferees considered the Sarvodaya experience, wondering what can be learned from it in finding a value system that can unite and empower people in both underdeveloped and mal-developed societies.

In many ways, of course, Sarvodaya's experience is culture-specific: the language and constructs it uses to mobilize people derive from Buddhism; its strategies for action are geared to a pre-industrial society. We cannot all go cut a road through the jungle, or organize our community through the local monk. In what ways, then, can its experience be applicable and meaningful to the rest of us? Are there lessons we can draw from it? As one who attended the Enschede meeting and who is active in social-change movements in the United States, I believe there are many such lessons. From these five—to begin with— we can learn:

TO LISTEN TO THE PEOPLE

Ariyaratna says, "A country cannot develop unless one has faith in the intelligence of the people." How is this intelligence tapped?

It was with the villagers first and foremost, not the urban elite or government officials, that Ariyaratna and his colleagues sought to communicate; and since true communication is a two-way street, that meant listening, too. To listen with attention and respect is a skill which the Movement stressed, emphasizing that it is the villagers themselves who are, in the last analysis, the "experts" on what they need and what they can do. Instead of coming in with preformulated blueprints for action, organizers, as we have seen, instigate "family gatherings" where the local community itself assesses its needs and determines its priorities by consensus. These provide, sometimes for the first time, the occasion where a broad cross-section of villagers can listen to each other, too. Out of this interaction has grown the fresh and deceptively simple formulations through which Sarvodaya conveys its philosophy of development.

A striking feature of the many Sarvodaya organizers I knew was their respect for the common man, woman, or child at the grassroots level. They appeared able to see value in each person's experience and perspective, whatever his background or extent of formal schooling. Their ability to do so—to perceive and accord value—may be reinforced by the Sarvodayan practice of *metta*, the lovingkindness meditation which breeds respect for all beings; but, in any case, it has permitted people in over four thousand villages to feel that they count and that they have some kind of ownership in Sarvodaya's programs.

In my own country many concerned and well-intentioned people do not act on social problems, because they feel they do not have the "answers" to them. Sarvodaya reminds us that prefabricated solutions are unnecessary and even dysfunctional, and that what we really need to do is go to the people, generate communication, and be unafraid to listen.

TO INTEGRATE SPIRITUAL AND SOCIAL CHANGE

Sarvodaya's dynamism derives to a large extent, as we have seen, from its capacity to merge people's spiritual aspirations with engagement in community action. Seeking to "awaken" both person and society, its values aim for individual fulfillment as well as social transformation. Although I had expected otherwise, imagining that they resided mainly in headquarters rhetoric, I found these values to be vital and self-generating among grassroots workers. Their comments and behavior conveyed a simple, bold, matter-of-fact assumption that through engagement in Sarvodaya's programs, their fellow-beings can transform their experience of who they are and how they relate to each other. For most this belief is basic to a continuing personal commitment that has few, if any, material rewards.

Such a wholistic view of social change is pertinent to industrialized societies as well, where the old conceptual dichotomies that divided the personal and spiritual from the social and political are beginning to erode. In cultures plagued by alienation and despair there is a hunger for the sense of meaning, belonging, and hope that such an integration can bring. Indeed, there are many signs that it is occurring, in a convergence of concerns. The 1960s in America generated a surge of social reform efforts (in the civil rights and antiwar movements); the 1970s saw a shift to the search for more personal transformation (in the human potential and spiritual awareness movements). A convergence of these two currents is evident in the 1980s, as increasing numbers of people on the local level turn to concerns for peace and social justice, but within the context of spiritual growth. Religious beliefs are being rearticulated in social terms, as people seek guidance and support in reshaping their lives and their society.

TO RESTORE COLLECTIVE SELF-ESTEEM

A third lesson to derive from Sarvodaya relates to the universal human need for identity and continuity. Roots are as necessary to people as to plants; for without a sense of the past, of the momentum and connection it provides, there can be little sense of future. Ariyaratna clearly appreciated this need; for instead of presenting his Movement as a novel endeavor, or taking credit for it as his own innovative idea, he did just the opposite. He rooted Sarvodaya in his people's past, offering it as something familiar but momentarily forgotten. Linking it with the distant glories of ancient Ceylon, evoking Dhanagara and Dharmadveepa through the speeches he gave and the songs he wrote, he restored his people's memory of that lost time. Reaching back behind today's poverty and itch to emulate the modern West, back beyond the dislocations and humiliations of the colonial period, he gave them a past to take pride in—and helped them, thereby, feel more adequate to the future.

The retelling of history can enrich it and make it more relevant to present needs, as we let it reflect those qualities in us that we choose to value. Just as each society has had its humiliations, violence, and "just wars", so can each find in its past early traditions of, for example, voluntary labor-sharing—though many in our modern world, where labor is regarded as a commodity and disutility, have forgotten these medieval or frontier customs. When Ariyaratna heard about church-sponsored work camps in Europe, he instituted his own Sri Lankan version in 1958 and coined the term "shramadana." The shramadana camp, as we have seen, initiated the Sarvodaya Movement and remains its central community-organizing strategy. What I would stress here is that Ariyaratna presented it to the people not as a novelty or Western import, but as rooted in their proud and distinctive past. He has been so successful in helping his people appropriate this method as their own that virtually everyone I consulted referred to shramadana as an old Ceylonese custom. "We have always done shramadana; that is the Sri Lankan way," they say with legitimate pride.

The need for a sense of national pride is evident throughout the world as the old orders break down and groups struggle to reclaim their distinctive identity, allegiance—and even moral righteousness. The new fundamentalisms, such as the Islamic Brotherhood in the Middle East or the Moral Majority in the United States, testify to the power of this need; and it cannot be assuaged by material goods, for it extends beyond economics to a people's sense of their own unique character and purpose. When thwarted or misguided, it can turn pathological, tearing the social fabric; but the need itself is legitimate. It is palpable in my country, where domestic and world crises breed a maddening sense of powerlessness and humiliation, and a new jingoism results in movements of the far right.

There is much energy in this need for national pride and, as the Sarvodaya experience dramatizes, it can be tapped in positive, socially constructive ways. Just as Sarvodaya drew on Ceylonese history, modifying it to make cooperation and sharing a source of pride, so can we. Voluntarism and mutual self-help, for example, are intrinsic to American history too, and can with justification be presented as the bedrock of the American character.

Sarvodaya's experience also reminds us that national pride can go hand in hand with international solidarity and cooperation. A society that is secure in its own self-esteem is less inclined to fear or resent others, or to cast itself in the role of victim or victimizer. As I and many other foreign visitors to Sarvodaya recognized, self-respect on the local level nourishes rather than inhibits a sense of world community—or *vishvodaya*, world awakening.

TO UNDERTAKE JOINT WORK PROJECTS

A primary way that Sarvodaya enlists people in development efforts is through presenting them with the opportunity and challenge to *give*. It is through giving, especially in an open, interactive situation, that they build their self-esteem and self-reliance. An individual's most personal, universal and unalienable possession is not money or goods, but his energy (*shrama*), or labor, time, and experience; and the Movement, as we saw in some detail in Chapter IV, creates occasions for him to offer *shrama* to his community and to experience its value.

There are a number of ways, as I learned from many a shrama-dana camp, that the sharing of physical labor serves to empower people, the accomplishment of a given task being only one of them:

1. It builds solidarity, cutting through the social and political divisions within a community in a way that seldom happens when interaction remains on the verbal level alone. It is harder to dismiss or stereotype a person whose views or background may differ from yours, once you have built a road—or even a bookcase—together, for the experience itself generates mutual trust and respect.

2. It focuses a community's attention on the physical and social conditions in which they live. The process of selecting and planning a common work project raises consciousness, as local people confront

their own situation, discuss it together, and begin to take responsibility for it.

3. It evokes and instills community leadership skills. In the process of organizing the work project, men, women, and even children discover and develop their abilities to motivate and coordinate contributions of time, tools, food, and labor.

4. It emboldens people to speak out. Those who have been more passive, apathetic, or timid are more likely to share their views with other members of the community after they have physically labored together.

5. It bestows a sense of ownership.

> When the government builds a school or community center, people have gone in the night to steal the hinges off the doors; but when people build by shramadana, nothing is touched—they even go repair it, as if it were their own house."
>
> *(School principal)*

These functions and values of shared labor projects are not limited to Sri Lanka and other Third World societies. Opportunities to work together as a community exist in industrialized countries as well, from the rehabilitation of urban housing to the creation of neighborhood gardens. Indeed, in those settings such ventures offer additional rewards, for they help people break out of the isolation and anonymity characteristic of modern society, and out of the sense of powerlessness bred by dependence on high technology. Many such projects are being undertaken in the "neighborhood power" movement in the United States, as local people rediscover the value of "doing-it-yourself... together."

The Sarvodaya experience teaches that the sense of community these projects create can be enhanced by gatherings where, in addition to the sharing of labor, people also share food, ideas, entertainment, and prayers. The work serves as pretext and context for these other empowering interactions. The Movement's shramadanas are like a combination of road gang, picnic, town meeting, vaudeville show, and revival service—and these many facets build people's trust and enjoyment of each other. The religious component serves to integrate people's energies, inspiring them with a sense of continuity with the society's core values and attracting the more traditional and pious elements, those who might otherwise consider the project irrelevant or "newfangled." While Sarvodaya's work camps derive motivation predominantly from Buddhism, they are undertaken in the context of other faiths as well, for all major religions extol the virtues of self-offering in service to others. As a Muslim district coordinator expressed it: "How do you think Mohammed rebuilt Medina? By shramadana, of course."

TO ENGAGE THE YOUNG

From the outset Ariyaratna chose to work with and through the young in challenging his society to "awaken." The first shramadana was led by sixteen- and seventeen-year-old students; and all the shramadanas and projects that followed focused on the powerless elements of society, which include not only women and the landless and poor, but school dropouts and little children as well. Today the Movement's "Children's Services," which institute preschools and attendant health and nutrition activities, are a chief Sarvodaya program—often the first to be initiated in a village; and the *Youn Haule* (Youth Group) for teen-agers and young adults is often the first Sarvodaya group to be established in a locality. Visiting a Sarvodaya project, one is struck by their presence and the role they play.

Some foreign observers view Sarvodaya's programs for the young as a social service which the Movement undertakes because it is a relatively easy and noncontroversial one. When I had been there for a while, I realized that these programs, particularly the preschool, served as an opening wedge for community organizing, recruiting the mothers and then enlisting families. Only after having participated in Sarvodaya activities for a longer time did I begin to take seriously its motivating philosophy—that one builds *janashakti* (people's power) not only from the grassroots up, but also from the infant up. I saw teen-age dropouts organize village shramadanas. I saw them conduct house-to-house surveys which not only recruited people to participate, but offered the first economic analysis of a village. I saw ten- and twelve-year-old children take responsibility for supplying tea and water to the work camp . . . and even younger children performing skits and songs which transmitted, better than any politician's speeches, the old values of cooperation, discipline, and self-reliance. In village after village I saw the commitment and idealism of the children drawing adults into the Movement. Proud of their offspring and challenged by them, parents, aunts, and uncles began to participate in Sarvodaya and assume responsibilities themselves.

> What strikes me most [after a visit to Sri Lanka] is that Sarvodaya does not regard unemployed youth as a liability—as most societies do, where they are a drain on the economy and can be volatile and destructive. Somehow Sarvodaya has been able to turn them into an asset.
>
> (*World Bank official*)

This facet of Sarvodaya's experience has obvious relevance to other societies, and especially to industrialized countries where youth suffer from unemployment and a sense of meaninglessness and superfluity. They want to make an impact; and when channels for constructive, responsible activity are not available to them, they make an impact in other ways—through violence, vandalism, and a variety of cults. The same energies could go into reforesting our depleted lands or running the postal service. The idealism and energy are there, in the young, as Sarvodaya has recognized and gambled on. The Movement enlists them in the reawakening of rural Sri Lanka. It recruits them to build harmony between the conflicting ethnic communities of Tamils and Sinhalese. It trusts them to serve on its Village Councils, whose composition must include not only farmers, mothers, young adults, and teen-agers, but also representatives from the *Singiti Haule* (Children's Group), who now sit with their elders to contribute their views and share responsibility for community development.

In such ways, then, can the Sarvodaya Shramadana Movement in Sri Lanka have meaning for other societies. It has meaning not because it embodies an ideal, as if its participants were all virtuous and noble. The Movement, like all other organizations, is amply beset with human failings; it suffers, as do we all, from delusion, greed, sloth, conflict. Indeed, that makes its story more relevant, for it shows how people can work together for development despite all the obstacles of our obstinate humanity. What it shows, particularly, is that we can learn to draw strength from each other, and especially from the religious traditions to which we are heir. Powerless, embittered, and apathetic Sri Lankan villagers have drawn inspiration for action from their once-discredited tradition, the Dharma. If that is so—and it is—then people the world over can find power, too, in their religious traditions. Each of them—Judaism, Islam, Christianity, Hinduism—offers resources for the development of person and society.

IX

Sarvodaya in the Mid-Eighties: An Update

R EPORTS OF CIVIL CONFLICT BEGAN TO DOMINATE NEWS FROM Sri Lanka soon after the year I spent there gathering the experiences on which the previous chapters are based. Eruptions of terrorist activity on the part of secessionist elements among the Tamil minority and repressive counter-measures by the Sinhalese-dominated government pre-empted domestic and international attention. The tragic conflict exacts a high toll in human suffering, and threatens to tear Sri Lanka apart.

With the purpose of discovering how this conflict has affected the Sarvodaya Shramadana Movement and how the Movement embodies Buddhist-inspired ideals in this situation of polarization and violence, I returned to Sri Lanka in the winter and again in the fall of 1984. Other questions preoccupied me as well. I wanted to learn what has happened to the Movement's plans to decentralize. I wondered whether these plans had been disrupted by the civil conflict and whether they had succeeded in generating autonomous village structures.

As in my earlier research in 1979 and 1980, I did not go with either the intention or the capacity to evaluate the Sarvodaya Shramadana Movement as a development agency. Rather I went to study the uses it made of indigenous spiritual values in defining what development is and in motivating people to take charge of their lives. As before, I wanted to know how these values can be evoked and applied in periods of stress. And now the stresses were very clear. They are similar to those experienced around the globe and in our own societies, as we cope with rising levels of conflict while searching for ways to increase the power people can exert over their own lives.

SARVODAYA AND THE CIVIL CONFLICT

Background of the Conflict

The conflict now tearing at Sri Lanka is rooted in historical forces that set the island's two major ethnic communities in competition with each other for economic opportunity and political self-determination. One of them, 74% of the island's population, is Sinhalese; its culture and language (Sinhalese) and its religion (mainly Buddhism, the faith of almost 90% of the Sinhalese) are the dominant strands in the fabric of Sri Lankan history. The largest minority (12%) is the population known as Ceylonese Tamil, deriving from ancient incursions and settlements from Southern India, and based largely in the northern and northeastern reaches of the island. Its language and culture (Tamil) and its religion (Hindu) are distinct from those of the Buddhist Sinhalese majority with whom it has shared millenia of the island's history. This common history includes long periods of peaceful coexistence and cooperation, and also occasional confrontations when Sinhalese and Tamil kings did battle.*

The British, during their century-and-a-half of colonial rule, favored this minority, giving it access to positions in the civil service; and so did American missionaries, establishing quality schools that gave the Tamils a competitive edge over the Sinhalese. Due to these developments and by dint of their own diligence, the Ceylonese Tamils gained a favorable position in the legal and medical professions as well as administrative posts, enjoying, I was informed, 40% to 50% of "certifiable" jobs throughout the country.

Such disproportionate representation in the more desirable jobs was resented by the Sinhalese—and when independence was gained in 1948, this resentment took the form of policy implemented by the ruling Sinhalese majority. Sinhalese was proclaimed the national language. Quotas were established, along with intricate grading systems, to allow Sinhalese to enter universities and government service in numbers commensurate with their population—moves not dissimilar to "affirmative action" measures in the United States. Furthermore, the national government invested relatively little in the arid northern zones where most Tamils lived.

---

*In addition to the Ceylonese Tamils, there are also 800,000 "estate Tamils," also known as "Indian Tamils," a population deriving from the low-caste laborers the British brought in from India to work on the tea and rubber estates. Though many are still stateless, most of those who can vote have supported the majority Sinhalese government. During recent disturbances many estate Tamils suffered at the hands of Sinhalese gangs. Their situation and aspirations, however, are not to be confused with those of the Ceylonese Tamils.

The Tamils chaffed under these policies that they, naturally enough, considered discriminatory. Finding little leverage in the Parliamentary process, where they were consistently outvoted, a minority among them began to call for secession and the establishment of an independent state called Eelam. Given its size, location and natural resources, the projected Eelam was considered by few, even among Ceylonese Tamils, as a realistic or viable option. Demands for its establishment seemed largely symbolic, but as the situation polarized, they took on increasing reality.

Separatist elements in the North, spawning guerrilla groups known as "Tamil Tigers," attacked police and military posts and personnel which, being largely Sinhalese, were viewed as an army of occupation. These terrorist acts in turn fueled Sinhalese fears and intransigence. These fears were also exacerbated by the promotion of the Eelam cause by influential Ceylonese Tamils living overseas, including many in the United States. The Sinhalese, though domestically in the vast majority, began to see themselves as a beleaguered minority. They see the secessionists receiving aid, arms and encouragement from overseas Tamils and even, reportedly, paramilitary training in Tamil Nadu, the nearby South Indian state with whom Ceylonese Tamils have cultural, linguistic and religious ties. They consider that the Ceylonese Tamils have a homeland in India, while they as Sinhalese have no homeland but Sri Lanka and no other base for their proud, pure heritage of Sinhalese Buddhism.

Large-scale violence erupted in July 1983, when Tamil Tigers ambushed and killed 13 Sinhalese members of the Sri Lankan military. The Sinhalese backlash unleased nationwide riots that destroyed Tamil property and claimed hundreds, if not thousands, of Tamil lives. The atrocities committed during that tragic week still traumatize the nation, feeding a desperation on both sides that is reinforced with each progressive act of terrorism and police control. In the absence of a realistic manner of dealing with Tamil demands for autonomy within the context of a unitary state, the downward spiral of attack, retaliation, reprisal and repression continues increasing the enormous cost in human lives and hopes.

Sarvodaya's Response

As pointed out in Chapter Two, the Movement is religiously and culturally pluralistic; it works among Tamils as well as Sinhalese, among Hindus, Christians and Muslims as well as the Buddhist majority, enlisting clerics and using the teachings of all faith systems. Yet it is a Buddhist-inspired movement, born in the Buddhist South, which prominently features Buddhist monks and whose predominant symbols and concepts are drawn from the Buddha Dharma. In spite of this largely Buddhist identification, Sarvodaya has been able to work to mitigate the hostilities.

When the July 1983 riots broke out, with Sinhalese gangs looting and burning Tamil quarters in Colombo and sparking similar rampages across the country, Sarvodaya's leader, A.T. Ariyaratna was the first national voice to call for calm and order. When he did not succeed in persuading the President to intervene publicly and immediately (President Jayewardene remained silent during the first half-week of the rioting), Ariyaratna himself went on the air to appeal to the people for compassion and restraint.

When the July 1983 riots broke out, with Sinhalese gangs looting and burning Tamil quarters in Colombo and sparking similar rampages across the country, Sarvodaya's leader, A.T. Ariyaratna was the first national voice to call for calm and order. When he did not succeed in persuading the President to intervene publicly and immediately (President Jayewardene remained silent during the first half-week of the rioting), Ariyaratna himself went on the air to appeal to the people for compassion and restraint.

The violence continued to escalate as goon squads, apparently incited by right wing Sinhalese political interest, began to claim the lives as well as the property of Tamils—and to threaten those who would give them refuge. Many Sinhalese of goodwill stood helplessly by, fearful of risking their own homes and families; but Sarvodaya workers, almost as if they had been trained for such emergency, proceeded without hesitation to secure as best they could the safety of the Tamils. Though mobs hammered at the gates of Damsak Mandir, the Movement's headquarters outside of Colombo, it became a haven for frightened Tamils, as did many a Sarvodaya center across the country.

While Sarvodayans were not the only ones to intervene—for other individuals in the Sinhalese community also took action to assist the Tamils—Sarvodaya as a Movement was able to act swiftly and cohesively because of its previous intercommunal work. Not only had its shramadanas and family gatherings built habits of trust, but also in the immediately preceding years and months the Movement had undertaken specific measures. In 1981, '82 and '83, it had organized a series of "Amity Camps" where several hundred Sinhalese and Tamil young people, in equal numbers, journeyed to selected sites to live and work together for two weeks. There they arranged exchange visits in each others' homes and villages; some of these visits were underway when the riots occurred.

By the end of the week of riots in July 1983, Ariyaratna and his coworkers had set up, staffed and supplied a temporary refugee camp for eight thousand Tamils in Ratmalana, between Colombo and Sarvodaya headquarters. That original camp is virtually disbanded, as Tamils of the Colombo area have returned to their homes or gone north; but other refugee camps initiated by the Movement are still in operation. I visited two of them in 1984. I talked with the Sinhalese and Tamil

Sarvodayans who staff them, saw the dwellings, preschools and collective gardens created by Shramadana. I saw the efforts to rebuild the lives of the dispossessed through the technical training that Sarvodaya can offer and the assistance and loans it can mediate from government sources and foreign agencies.

Sarvodaya's organization and methods enable it to carry out relief and rehabilitation work without undue difficulty. The Movement has also undertaken more problematic initiatives to help resolve the political conflict and to attempt to affect the attitudes on both sides so that a resolution may be possible.

Shortly after the riots, Ariyaratna journeyed in person to Jaffna, the Tamil city in the north which is the center of secessionist activity. He was the first Sinhalese public figure to go and was advised against it—for the country was still reeling from the recent bloodshed. There was fear for his safety, but he saw his trip as a move conducive to sanity, to demonstrate that Sri Lankans could still trust each other. Thousands of Ceylonese Tamils flocked to hear and meet him.

Then, in further moves to defuse the crisis and promote Sarvodaya's ideals of nonviolence and unity, he called a national conference to be held on Gandhi's birthday, October 2, 1983, prepared for its deliberations a "Declaration on National Peace and Harmony," and announced a subsequent hundred-day Peace Walk which would march from one end of the island to the other, from the Buddhist South to the Tamil North, enlisting members of all communities.

These actions took place in an atmosphere of growing polarization. The majority community laid virtually all the blame for the conflict and the riots on the Tamils and found it very difficult to acknowledge any responsibility at all for the current impasse. Its statements and behaviours increasingly reflected a Buddhist Sinhalese nationalism in which the history, character and mission of Sri Lanka are identified with Sinhalese Buddhism. Such a view is encouraged by ancient chronicles like the Mahavamsa. Accorded the status of sacred scripture, the chronicles portray Sri Lanka as specifically designated by the Buddha himself as a repository for pure Buddhism, to be secured and protected from the depredations of lesser beings, namely the Dravidian peoples from whom issue the present-day Tamils. This nationalism, with its racist overtones, is expressed today by many high-placed members of the Sangha.

To such views the declaration prepared by Ariyaratna and publicized at the conference presented a courageous contrast. It blamed the conflict not on the Tamils but on the destruction of Sri Lanka's indigenous value system. It described this value system as "founded on the ancient Hindu-Buddhist Code of Ethics," and it said that, in view of the fact that the world's media thrust responsibility for the riots on the Sinhalese Buddhists, this portion of the Sri Lankan public must bear the "onus of responsibility" for redeeming the situation.

Instead of denigrating persons and communities, the declaration addressed the values which guide them, or rather the loss of values from which they suffer. The core value system that is to be upheld is not portrayed as Buddhist alone, but as shared with the Hindu Tamils. And yet the Buddhists themselves are called to account. I am aware of no other voice out of Sinhalese Buddhism that went this far.

Preparations for the Peace Walk, announced at the Conference inspired by Gandhi and Vinoba Bhave's marches in India, consumed the efforts of Sarvodaya leaders and organizers for two months. On December 6, 1983, thousands gathered at Kataragama, a pilgrimage site in the far south sacred to both Hindus and Buddhists. After extensive religious ceremonies, where some high clerics of different faiths participated in each others' rituals for the first time, the Peace Walk began, marching in solemn, white-clad silence the first day's journey of fifteen miles. It went no further. President Jayewardene met with the assembly that evening and recommended that the Walk be postponed. He had information, he said, that violence on the part of extremist elements was planned and that Ariyaratna's life was at risk; the turmoil that was likely to ensue would endanger the delicate negotiations of the All-Party Congress, just beginning its year-long deliberations. Ariyaratna conceded. The Walk disbanded.

The virtue of this decision not to proceed with the Peace Walk has been debated. It was suggested that the postponement, which was virtually cancellation, was an act of cowardice or subservience. Some Sarvodayans were angry, all were disappointed, but most now defend the decision. To continue the Walk, they argue, would have been an act of open defiance of the national government, which would have drawn into their ranks large numbers of political dissidents whose nonviolent conduct Sarvodaya could no way assure. The many Sarvodayans who would have joined the Walk proceeded to hold, in each town along its projected route, assemblies dedicated to peace and amity. And gradually their energies reverted to the grassroots development efforts that are central to the Movement. Yet, as we see below, this was not a return to the *status quo ante*.

Impact of the Conflict on Sarvodaya

Sarvodaya's responses to the crisis has affected its image in the public eye. Sinhalese who had previously dismissed the Movement as a well-meaning but a not very important form of do-goodism, expressed to me in 1984 a sober respect for the example and leadership it has provided in the civil emergency. Tamils with whom I talked in the North were more open to the Movement than ever before, seeing it as a legitimate expression of the people as a whole and, as more than one said to me, "our only hope."

Sarvodaya's response has also aroused anger and suspicion. Tamil separatists, as well as some foreign observers and even donors to the Movement, have charged the Movement with not giving adequate attention to Tamil claims and grievances. They point to the clear allegiance, expressed in Ariyaratna's Declaration for Peace and Harmony, to the concept of a "unitary state," thereby rejecting any serious consideration of secession. Subsequent statements by Sarvodaya leadership, they also point out, refrain from specifically denouncing oppressive government policies or indiscriminate acts of retaliation by Sinhalese police and military forces.

Sarvodaya has been subject to criticism from the other side as well. Right-wing elements among the majority population, who identify Sri Lanka's survival with the hegemony of Sinhalese Buddhism, see Sarvodaya as "soft" on Tamils. They tend to suspect the Movement of betraying the essentially Sinhalese Buddhist character of the state. Such attitudes arising from extremist factions within the Sinhalese Buddhist present more of a danger to Sarvodaya and its leadership than do exasperations on the part of the Tamils. Mahatma Gandhi, we recall, died at the hands of fanatical elements in his own religious community. It was to such a danger that President Jayewardene alluded in recommending that Sarvodaya cancel the Peace Walk.

Whatever one's judgment of Sarvodaya's role in the crisis, the fact remains that it is the only voluntary nationwide organization in which both Sinhalese and Tamils continue to work together. Indeed, more Tamils are involved in the Movement than ever before. They include Ceylonese Tamils in positions of responsibility as District Coordinators and Gramodaya organizers, as well as those participating in village-level Sarvodaya Societies. Their numbers are not tallied since the Movement does not tabulate its members according to ethnic origin, but the Field Director for the North estimates the recent increase in Tamil participation in Sarvodaya to be tenfold. There are also now more "estate Tamils" taking part in the Movement; among them and on the plantations where they work, Sarvodaya has increased its nutritional, health, technical and educational programs.

Even at Sarvodaya Headquarters in the Buddhist South I detected a difference. There I found on my last visit fifty Tamil schoolteachers using the premises for an inservice training program sponsored by the Ministry of Education. The site was chosen with a reason. "We feel safer here," several of them commented to me, "safer even than in Jaffna." In Jaffna, the center of Tamil secessionist activity in the North, moderate Tamils now experience as much if not more danger from guerrilla attacks as do the Sinhalese military and police forces.

My old friend Jothi, a Sinhalese, is now District Coordinator in the Amparai region in the east, where there are also many Tamils and an increase in terrorist activity. "After four o'clock no one ventures on the roads," he said, "for fear of the Tigers' attacks. But the Sarvodaya jeep can go. No problem. Everyone knows we serve all the people without taking sides; we are trusted." Some of the local Tamils active in their village Sarvodaya Societies have confidentially identified themselves to Jothi as "Tigers;" but they persist in Sarvodaya work because it makes sense, because it is needed, and perhaps because it represents an island of sanity in a polarized world.

"Sarvodaya means 'waking up' to what we have in common," said my friend Hewa, another District Coordinator. "We face hunger and disease and unemployment. Both Sinhalese and Tamils face this suffering. What is important is that we talk together and meet these problems together and not let the politicians set us against each other."

I had, previous to my return, wondered whether Sarvodaya's effectiveness in working for reconciliation was limited by its largely Buddhist identification. I found, on the contrary, that its relation to Buddhism enables the Movement to play a distinctive and critical role; for it presents an understanding and experience of the Dharma that is consonant with a pluralistic society. At a time when the Buddhist Sinhalese majority is tempted to adopt a narrowly defensive posture, identifying Sri Lanka as a Buddhist Sinhalese state, Sarvodaya demonstrates the tolerance and respect for diversity that are integral to the teachings of the Buddha. To Gautama, the notion that one could be in possession of an absolute truth or of exclusive historical privileges was a dangerous delusion, an occasion for attachment, aversion and ignorance, and the suffering they engender. Sarvodaya from the outset incorporated this recognition and exercised it by including members of all faiths and communities. So it is now able to offer to the Sri Lankan Buddhist majority a way of being true to the Dharma while working actively for the needs and rights of all beings without falling prey to Buddhist nationalism.

THE DECENTRALIZATION OF SARVODAYA

In 1980 the Sarvodaya Movement began an effort designed to give more control over program and budgetary decisions to the district and village level structures it had created. This struck me at the time as an unusual move. Power in organizations tends to accumulate at the center and rarely is it deliberately relinquished in favor of those at the periphery. On my return visits in 1984 I was eager to see whether and how this process was actually being implemented, especially in light of the tensions created by the Tamil-Sinhalese conflict. It would be natural, I knew, for central control to tighten in a period of violence and danger, when the rank and file are under pressures of confusion and fear.

I arrived back to find that the Headquarters had grown yet larger. The new buildings at Damsak Mandir, the ubiquitous pictures of Ariyaratna, the frequent references to "our leader" and the reverential celebrations of his birthday, all can prompt the casual visitor to wonder about the extent to which power in Sarvodaya is or can be decentralized.

Ariyaratna was absent during my last visit to Headquarters and I was able to see how decisions are made, programs undertaken, emergencies handled while "the leader" is away. I was also able as before to spend time in the field and see the initiatives taken in the Movement's district, divisional and village-level activities.

At the Grassroots

In operation now on the grassroots level is the Sarvodaya Shramadana Society, a structure that in 1980 was only in idea form. Now numbering over 2000, these village-based societies represent an evolution and integration of previously existing local groups. The villagers, whom I had earlier seen working together in shramadana camps and creating mothers' groups, youth groups, elders' groups, etc., now constitute themselves as a legal corporate body in their locality, enrolling as members and paying modest dues. Legal incorporation is important because it enables them to have their own bank account, control their own funds, buy land and equipment, apply for grants, enter into bilateral loan agreements and employ people. It means even more psychologically; it encourages initiative and self-respect. It also encourages savings and mutual responsibility in using these savings. Here a Sarvodaya Society has created a milk-collecting cooperative; there it has invested collectively in an irrigation pump, carefully monitoring its use; in another village it has pooled resources to buy seed and fertilizer; in another it has sought and received government assistance in acquiring materials for housing construction. In each case the Society can now act as a responsible and independent agency. Its Executive Council must include, along with the farmers and elders, a minimum of three women, three youth and three children.

The proviso ensuring the participation of women, youth and children in these Societies is a telling reflection of Sarvodaya's methods and goals. These are the traditionally powerless ones. And, as before, I was struck by the activities engendered for them and by them in the Movement.

Children play a significant role in Sarvodaya, a more central one than in other development organizations with which I am familiar. The Movement uses their needs—for preschools, nutrition and health attention—to begin to organize in a community. Their songs and skits help propagate Sarvodaya values; their energy and commitment enliven the Shramadana camps. Under the guidance of Sarvodaya organizers, they work in the community gardens and market the produce in children's fairs; with the profit, they undertake and sustain savings schemes which serve in turn as an example for their families and their communities.

Recently in India, I visited villages where Gandhian workers had been organizing for years. I was struck by the fact that it was the adults who displayed and took credit for the improvements, while the village children gathered around the fringes of the group as curious spectators. The expensive concrete latrines, built by the government to government specifications, remained unused. Perhaps next year, I was told, the village people will be organized to learn to use them. I recalled the latrines built by shramadana in Sri Lanka, with their economical thatched walls, and with the children helping to canvas the community and to carry the pans of excavated dirt and making skits and songs about it all at the family gatherings. That kind of participation and local pride ensured that the latrines were *used*. And I appreciated afresh both the cultural component that the Sarvodaya Shramadana Movement brings to development work and its cleverness in recruiting children as agents of social change.

The role of women in Sarvodaya, while inseparable to some extent from that of the children, appears to be even more significant. As I described in Chapter Seven, women constitute the backbone of the Movement's village-level programs and projects. The Sarvodaya-trained preschool teachers are the Movement's cutting edge, often the first to create new structures and programs in a given village. Working through the children, they recruit the mothers; working the the mothers, they establish community kitchens and health services. The Movement's recent programs — creating community shops and introducing alternative technology, like Sarvodaya's new, fuel-efficient stoves — all rely to a substantial degree on the preschool teachers and the mothers' groups they organize.

The commitment and endurance of these young women is central to the local self-reliance that Sarvodaya aims to generate. Some observers of the Movement have criticized it for its acceptance of, and apparent dependence upon large infusions of foreign aid; they have questioned whether Sarvodaya could sustain its activities without this external assistance. One cannot tell if these fears are valid since donors continue to support the Movement; but the last year offers a partial answer. In early 1984 cutbacks in foreign assistance to Sarvodaya severely curtailed its program funds and the Movement terminated the minimal allowances it had offered its preschool teachers. It was feared by some that this would result in the loss of these women organizers. Yet virtually all of them have continued. According to the 1984 Annual Report, 2475 Sarvodaya preschool teachers and 353 community health workers (also mainly women) are continuing to work without any allowance and 1934 have managed to generate regular financial support from their own villages.

As the Movement has decentralized, a new level of local organization has appeared: the Gramadana unit. This is the name for the Sarvodaya village whose full-time worker undertakes to organize ten additional, surrounding villages, helping them in turn to create Sarvodaya Societies. For eighteen months the Movement provides the Gramadana workers a minimal allowance; after that period the Societies they have organized are expected to assume responsibility for their wages. This expectation is partly based upon the ability the preschool teachers have demonstrated in securing local financial support even from among the less favored elements of the society. These Gramadana organizers are in many cases women, seasoned by the developmental responsibilities they were led into as preschool teachers and health workers and by the leadership training afforded them by the Movement.

Local initiative is also fostered by the systematic approach Sarvodaya has adopted in its process of decentralization. One of the first activities undertaken by the local Society upon incorporation (and often before incorporation) is an extensive survey of the villager's resources and needs, family by family, house by house. This inquiry into their standard of living—their employment, income, housing, clothing, diet, health, access to clean water, fresh vegetables, sanitation and other necessities—is now guided by an exhaustive and simply worded questionnaire supplied by the Movement and used by local members of all ages to survey the community. While it is designed primarily to help the local Society set goals and priorities for its work, the very process of the survey is beneficial to the community for it represents a process of consciousness-raising—or "conscientizacion," to borrow the term coined by Paolo Freire—which awakens people to the reality of their present situation and to a sense of mutual responsibility in meeting it.

Mid-Level Leadership

The most evident shift in Sarvodaya's internal power structure appeared to me to be at the level of the District Coordinators. The organization is divided geographically into some 25 Districts under the charge of Coordinators, mainly young men in their thirties who grew up with the Movement. The decentralization process has given them more responsibility and encouraged them to take more initiative. They run most of the trainings and educational programs offered by Sarvodaya—from preschool and health work to technical skills and community organizing and leadership. They can and do enter into bilateral agreements with other organizations, government programs and international aid agencies. They develop their own revenue sources undertaking income-generating projects, they raise and spend funds, hire personnel and administer loans. Some of them travel abroad to represent Sarvodaya to foreign governments and private agencies. They meet monthly at Sarvodaya Headquarters to review and coordinate their plans.

In 1984 their capacity to take initiative was increased with the designation of five Field Directors. These are District Coordinators who assume responsibility for advising and supervising other Coordinators in adjacent districts, assisting them with the development of their programs and resources. As well as attending the Coordinators' regular meetings, these five have their own monthly sessions with the Executive Director, where they look at the problems and opportunities facing the Movement as a whole and make recommendations for Sarvodaya's overall policy and budget.

Knowing several of these Field Directors and Coordinators long and well, I am struck by the vigor and seriousness with which they have grown into their increased responsibilities. Their pride in their own independent endeavors seems to go hand in hand with an undiminished loyalty and even reverence for Ariyaratna as their leader and teacher. They frequently refer to their relationship to him as one of *sheshya* (disciple) to *guru* (master, teacher).

"I stopped the Peace Walk because our leader said so, and I obey him," says one Coordinator. And in the next breath he says, "I could be making a decent salary in Government service or in business – even turned down a high-paying job last year. The reason I am working with Sarvodaya is because of the freedom it gives me. I have a lot of ideas and I can put them into action – fast, without red tape."

In India I interviewed a young administrator in a Gandhian institution who had served with the Sarvodaya Shramadana Movement in Sri Lanka as a United Nations volunteer. I asked him what he brought back from his experience with Sarvodaya that influenced his current development work. "Confidence," he said. "Dr. Ariyaratna showed me that I can be a leader, and now I know that I too can create change for my people. He helped me find my own strength." Then he added, laughing, "Ariyaratna is a strong leader because he is so human. Look how he smokes cigarettes in public. Here in India a Gandhian leader would do it secretly."

It is common in organizations of this size for relations to become strained between the headquarters and the field, between those who are closer to power and those who are closer to the action. The latter become impatient with the bureaucracy and suspected intrigues of those ensconced at the head office. This is true of Sarvodaya as well.

Such tensions within Sarvodaya are compounded by differences in age, outlook and experience. The Headquarters is largely staffed by retired professionals and civil servants who, after early exposure to Sarvodaya in their youth, now return to serve full-time and, thanks to their pensions, can do so at little or no cost. But they return to find the Movement has changed. Instead of a small core of their own peers, they find all these youngsters who have risen through the ranks to positions of responsibility, whose experience is entirely in the field — and there is some reluctance to concede control to them. The experience of most of the Headquarters staff is not with community organizing in rural settings so much as with urban-based service organizations such as the Scouts or the Lions Club, and that colors their understanding and expectations of Sarvodaya. Some complain that the field workers are too radical and headstrong, and some of these in turn suspect them of bureaucratic obstructionism. Ariyaratna is open to criticism for not cutting through this and allaying the frustrations of his young field-workers; yet the present tensions may be an inevitable stage through which the Movement is passing as the power shifts.

Buddhist Monks in a Decentralized Sarvodaya

The internal restructuring of power has affected the role that Buddhist monks are playing in Sarvodaya. The bhikkus' orange robes are still evident at Sarvodaya functions, their voices still lead the chanting of sacred sutras at Sarvodaya gatherings, and many of the bhikku organizers I knew are still going strong, presiding over the community programs they initiated and bestowing upon the Movement the aura of traditional continuity and legitimacy. Yet there are fewer full-time Sarvodaya bhikkus than before.

This reduction in the number of Buddhist monks who are devoting themselves to Sarvodaya organizing is attributable to several factors. One is the death of the Venerable Gnanaseeha, the charismatic Sangha leader who organized the training of Sarvodaya bhikkus. Another is the conciliatory role that Sarvodaya has played in the Tamil-Sinhalese conflict which is uncomfortable for conservative and nationalist Buddhist elements in the Sangha. But it is also Sarvodaya's decentralization that has, to some measure, made full-time community organization within the movement less attractive to the monks.

They are reluctant to place themselves in a position of accountability to laymen and especially young laymen. And now District Coordinators and Gramodaya leaders are in charge of their respective areas. While many bhikkus may be prepared to work in collaboration with local laypeople, it is quite another matter to work under their direction — to answer to them for implementation of Sarvodaya programs and use of Sarvodaya resources.

The somewhat diminished role of the bhikkus is also a matter of ingrained assumptions about the exercise of power. As a Sarvodaya

Field Director explained to me, "The bhikkus are still important in getting Sarvodaya activities started in a village. They introduce Sarvodaya. They start the groups, they organize a shramadana or two. But when villagers take charge and organize their own Sarvodaya Societies, they operate by consensus. And that is hard for the monk. He is accustomed to being the voice of authority. At this point, when the village is ready to take off, the monk becomes not a help but a liability."

Revisiting the temples at Rambodagala and Baddegama and other Buddhist sites where Sarvodaya activity had been nurtured, I met again the monks I had known and admired and found them still active in development work. Yet I knew their role was less essential than before. The Movement no longer needed the legitimacy they could bestow. Sarvodaya was accepted now in its own right and was disseminating notions of power that, though in accord with the teachings of the Buddha, had not been incorporated into the attitudes and habits of the Sangha as a monastic institution.

Autonomy and Collaboration with the Government

From the time the Movement was launched in 1958, when a Rural Development Officer helped Ariyaratna conceive and organize the first shramadana camp in Kanatholuwa, Sarvodaya has sought to bridge the gap between government resources and village needs. It has, as we saw in Chapter Four, encouraged villagers to represent their needs directly to government personnel and to utilize government programs. By the same token, Sarvodaya has helped government ministries and extension agents become more familiar with and responsive to the realities at the grassroots level.

Sarvodaya's success over the years in mobilizing rural participation in development activities has inspired certain government programs (such as those of the Ministries of Rural Development and Youth Affairs) to adopt some of Sarvodaya's organizing techniques and language. Not only are there government-sponsored shramadanas, there are also now local government-sponsored bodies called Gramodaya (village-awakening) councils. In addition, Sarvodaya acceded to the Prime Minister's request to help with his ambitious Udagama or "model village" program and took responsibility for organizing its cultural and service components. As a result, some Sarvodaya field organizers, working closely with government personnel, appear to be operating in a semi-official capacity.

These developments have prompted some observers to wonder whether and to what extent Sarvodaya is in danger of being co-opted by the government. In the eyes of the Movement itself, collaboration by and with the government is a mixed blessing. As a District Coordinator said, "The problem is not that the government uses our language, our ideas. The problem is when it does not understand them or follow through on them. Then the words are empty."

Furthermore, collaboration with the government risks compromising Sarvodaya's essentially non-partisan posture and its reputation as an independent advocate of the poor. "It is nice to be able to pick up the phone or stop by the Kachcheri and get the ear of the A.G.A.," commented another District Coordinator. "But I get worried that the villagers may lump us together—Sarvodaya and the government or Sarvodaya and the U.N.P. [the United National Party, which is in power]. Then they begin to expect us to do things *for* them. And that makes it harder for them to become self-reliant."

By and large, it is the staff at Sarvodaya Headquarters, more than the field workers, who are favorably disposed to those programs which integrate Sarvodaya and government efforts. Yet, for both field and headquarters personnel, this issue continues to be seen within the context of Sarvodaya's primary goal. This goal, in their eyes, is the "awakening of all"—and "all" means civil servants and extension agents as well as the landless and the unemployed. Each is seen as endowed with the capacity to be liberated from greed, hatred and delusion and to participate in the creation of an enlightened society.

Collaboration with the government poses questions about the degree and sense of autonomy that local Sarvodaya Societies and programs enjoy—and, as mentioned above, some observers of the Movement express concerns about "co-optation." Others, after witnessing Sarvodaya's impact and watching the Movement in action across the country, ask: "Who is co-opting whom?"

Decentralization, Expansion and Local Power Elites

Despite current and expected reductions in foreign assistance, the Movement continues to increase the number of villages in which it works, the trainings it conducts, the Sarvodaya Societies it organizes. This growth, considered desirable by the Movement's top leadership, is now projected into the future with plans to double the number of villages involved, from 6000 to 12000, within the next years.

Locally initiated projects and locally based trainings need a good deal of guidance and supervision if they are to incorporate the experience the Movement has accumulated over the last quarter century. Such supervision is hard to provide when organizers' efforts are spread thin and programs are proliferated before they have been adequately tested on a pilot basis. After describing some of the brave new ventures local Sarvodaya Societies were undertaking, a District Coordinator said, "The trouble is they need more attention than we are able to give. They need information and connections and help resolving conflicts. You know, it takes more time, more work, to help people to make their own decisions than if you simply make those decisions for them."

The drive to decentralize, when coupled with expansion, encourages Sarvodaya organizers to work through those local figures who have already demonstrated the ability to marshall resources. Often it is members of the local power elite—such as the more educated and liberal-minded landowners—who take leading roles in the Sarvodaya Societies, and who with their property and prestige are invited and relied upon to further Sarvodaya programs. In Sarvodaya meetings, surveys and projects, many of them learn to listen to, and even consult, less favored members of the local community. The revolutionary character of the Movement is then to be discerned less in radical shifts of power than in the effect it has on the attitudes and behavior of these local elites.

Because of its readiness to work through existing structures of power, both governmental or private, the Movement is criticized for lacking a class analysis and giving inadequate recognition to inherent and insurmountable oppositions between the privileged and the poor. This criticism can, it seems, be leveled at many other social movements in regard to their relations with existing power structures. In India I put the question to Gandhians in community development work, "What do you do with the local landowners and merchants and with the Block Development Officers?" "We try to enlist them, to get them on our side," was the repeated answer. There, as in Sri Lanka, Gandhi-inspired efforts to return power to the people included *all* people and operated on the assumption that all can serve and change.

THE INSTITUTIONALIZATION OF SARVODAYA

In its decentralization, Sarvodaya has created structures that are less dependent than before on its top leadership and more capable of enduring through time. These structures, and the capacity of Sarvodayans to take responsibility at the district and grassroots levels, promise a partial response to the question that is often asked: "What will happen to the Movement after Ariyaratna?"

The Movement has been so identified with the charismatic figure of Ariyaratna that many observers have expressed concern as to whether Sarvodaya could survive him. There is even some criticism that he, in his early fifties, is not designating and grooming a successor.

The same question was asked of the Buddha 2500 years ago: "Who will be our teacher when you die? Tell us who will lead." But Gautama refrained, he named no one. He said, "The Dharma itself will be your guide." And a movement arose, enduring to this day, that has no Pope or Vatican and that is the most decentralist of the world's major religions.

That analogy is hardly meant to equate the former highschool teacher, A.T. Ariyaratna, with Gautama Siddhartha, the Buddha. It is meant to reflect that similar assumptions are at work in the transfer of power. If through one's efforts people are offered the inspiration and guidelines to become self-reliant, that affects the question of who is to succeed.

Instead of grooming a successor, Ariyaratna has increased the responsibility of Sarvodaya's many local and district leaders. Instead of claiming for the Movement the exclusive right to purvey its ideas and methods, he promotes their dissemination through whatever means are at hand. Such an approach is not very neat, nor does it provide guarantees. Perhaps, at his death, the institution of Sarvodaya Shramadana Movement in Sri Lanka will disintegrate. Perhaps, then, the work that he and his colleagues undertook will appear to have been to no avail. Or perhaps those who participated in it and those—like us—who learned from it, will incorporate its values, its experience in ongoing efforts toward the "awakening of all."

Glossary

A.G.A.: Assistant Government Agent
arthachariya: constructive activity
bhikku: Buddhist monk
dana: giving; gift; generosity, a cardinal Buddhist virtue
deshodaya: national awakening
dhanagara: treasurehouse of plenty ("Granary of the East")
Dharma: the teachings of the Buddha, the law of reality; Buddhists'
    name for their religion
dharmadveepa: Isle of Righteousness
gandhigram: A South Indian center, based on Gandhian thought and
    engaged in community development
gramodaya: village awakening
gram sevaka: government village-level extension agent
imam: Muslim prayer-leader
janashakti: people's power
karma: the self-modifying effect of one's actions and intentions;
    activity
karuna: compassion
kovil: Hindu temple
lungi: long wrap-around skirt
metta: lovingkindness
model village: village established or rehabilitated under government
    auspices
muditha: sympathetic joy, joy in the joy of others
nirvana: release from the realm of suffering
paticca samuppada: dependent co-arising, the Buddha's teaching of
    mutual causality

paule hamua: family gathering (also used for the village meeting "as a family")

priyavachana: kindly speech

prasad: devotional food offering (Hindu)

purushodaya: personal awakening

samanatmatha: the Buddha's teachings on equality

Sangha: the Buddhist monastic order

sarvodaya: the awakening of all

shramadana: sharing human energy; a collective labor project

Sinhalese: predominant ethnic group in Sri Lanka; its language

stupa: Buddhist reliquary mound

sutra: Buddhist scripture

swashakti: personal power

Tamil: ethnic group of South Indian origin and Hindu religion; its language

upekkha: impartiality; equanimity

vihara: Buddhist temple and/or monastic residence

vishvodaya: world awakening.

Bibliography

Ariyaratna, A. T. *A Struggle to Awaken*. Sri Lanka: Sarvodaya Shramadana Movement, 1978.

_____. *Collected Works*, Vol. I. Netherlands: Sarvodaya Research Institute, 1979.

_____. *Collected Works*, Vol. II. Netherlands: Sarvodaya Research Institute, 1980.

_____. *In Search of Development: Sarvodaya Effort to Harmonize Tradition with Change*. Moratuwa: Sarvodaya Press, 1981.

_____. *Whence, Wherefore? Whither?: Babbha Jatika Balavegaya*. Sri Lanka: Sarvodaya Shramadana Movement, 1978.

Brown, Lester. *The 29th Day*. New York: W.W. Norton, 1978.

Carter, John Ross (ed.). *Religiousness in Sri Lanka*. Colombo, Marga Institute, 1979.

Compton, J. L. *Participative Education Programming*. Cornell University for U.S.A.I.D., Washington, D.C., 1979 (unpublished).

Coombs, Philip H. (ed.). *Meeting the Basic Needs of the Rural Poor: The Integrated Community-Based Approach*. New York: Pergamon Press, 1980.

Dana. Journal of Sarvodaya Shramadana Movement, Moratuwa.

Davids, C. Rhys (ed. and trans.). *Dhammapada*. London: Oxford University Press, 1931.

Davids, T. W. Rhys (ed.). *Dialogues of the Buddha*. London: Routledge and Kegan Paul Ltd., 1973–1977.

de Silva, L. A. *Buddhism: Beliefs and Practices in Sri Lanka*. Colombo: Ecumenical Institute for Study and Dialogue, 1974.

Gombrich, Richard F. *Precept and Practice: Traditional Buddhism in the Rural Highlands of Ceylon*. Oxford: Clarendon Press, 1971.

Goulet, Denis. *Survival with Integrity: Sarvodaya at the Crossroads.* Colombo: Marga Institute, 1981.

Hewage, L. G. *Metta: Lovingkindness—The Buddhist Approach.* Colombo: Middle Path International, 1974.

Kantowsky, D. *Sarvodaya: The Other Development.* New Delhi: Vikas Publishing House Pvt. Ltc., 1980.

Macy, Joanna R. "Ethics of Dependent Co-Arising," *Journal of Religious Ethics.* Spring, 1979.

_____. "Janashakti: The People's Power," *Dana.* No. 7/8, Feb/March 80, pp. 19–20.

_____. "Shramadana: Giving Energy," *The Next Whole Earth Catalog,* New York: Random House, 1980.

_____. "Three Lessons in Awakening," *Dr. A. T. Ariyaratna Felicitation Volume.* Ratmalana: Sarvodaya Research Institute, 1981.

Marga Institute. *Religion and Development in Asian Societies.* Colombo: Marga Publishing, 1974.

Moore, Cynthia. *Paraprofessionals in Village-Level Development in Sri Lanka: The Sarvodaya Shramadana Movement.* Ithaca: Cornell University, 1981.

Obeyesekere, Gananath, Frank Reynolds, and Bardwell Smith. *The Two Wheels of Dhamma: Essays on the Theravada Traditions in India and Ceylon.* Chambersburg, Pennsylvania: American Academy of Religion, 1972.

Postel, Els, and Jake Schrijvers (ed.). *A Woman's Mind Is Longer Than A Kitchen Spoon.* Netherlands: Research Project on Women in Development, University of Leiden, 1980.

Rahula, Walpola. *The Heritage of the Bhikku.* New York: Grove Press Inc., 1974.

_____. *History of Buddhism in Ceylon.* Colombo, M. D. Gunasena and Co., Ltc., 1956.

Ratnapala, Nandesena. *Sarvodaya and the Rodiyas: The Birth of Sarvodaya.* Ratmalana: Sarvodaya Research Institute, 1979.

_____. *The Sarvodaya Movement: Self-Help Rural Development in Sri Lanka.* Essex, Connecticut: International Council for Educational Development, 1978.

Risseeuw, Carla. *The Wrong End of the Rope: Women Coir Workers in Sri Lanka.* Netherlands: Research Project on Women in Development, University of Leiden, 1980.

Sarkisyanz, E. *Buddhist Background of the Burmese Revolution.* The Hague: Martinus Nijhoff, 1965.

Sarvodaya Research Institute. *Community Participation in Rural Development: Study of Seven Selected Villages in Sri Lanka.* Dehiwela:

Sarvodaya Research Institute, 1978.

_____. *Integrated Rural Development: A People's Approach.* Ratmalana: Sarvodaya Research Institute, 1982.

_____. *Sarvodaya Study—Service in Sri Lanka: 1975–1976.* Colombo: Sarvodaya Research Institute, 1976.

Sarvodaya Shramadana Movement. Annual Service Report, 1980–81. Moratuwa: Sri Lanka, April, 1981.

_____. *Village Industries and Community Shops.* Moratuwa: Sarvodaya Shramadana Movement, October, 1979.

Schumacher, E. F. *Small Is Beautiful.* New York: Harper and Row, 1973.

Tinker, I., and M. B. Bramsen. *Women and World Development.* Washington, D.C.: Overseas Development Council, 1976.

Vijayatunga, J. *Grass For My Feet: Vignettes of Life in Sri Lanka.* Colombo: K. V. G. de Silva and Sons, 1974.